Negotiating Literacy Learning

Exploring the Challenges and Achievements of Struggling Readers

JANINE K. BIXLER
Mount Saint Mary College

Allyn & Bacon
is an imprint of

Boston   New York   San Francisco
Mexico City   Montreal   Toronto   London   Madrid   Munich   Paris
Hong Kong   Singapore   Tokyo   Cape Town   Sydney

Vice President and Executive Publisher: Jeffery W. Johnston
Senior Editor: Linda Ashe Bishop
Senior Managing Editor: Pamela D. Bennett
Senior Project Manager: Mary M. Irvin
Editorial Assistant: Demetrius Hall
Senior Art Director: Diane C. Lorenzo
Cover Designer: Jeff Vanik
Cover Image: Jupiter Images
Operations Specialist: Matthew Ottenweller
Director of Marketing: Quinn Perkson
Marketing Coordinator: Brian Mounts

For related titles and support materials, visit our online catalog at www.ablongman.com

Library of Congress Cataloging in Publication Data

Bixler, Janine K.
  Negotiating literacy learning: exploring the challenges and achievements of struggling readers, K-6/Janine K. Bixler.
    p. cm.
  Includes bibliographical references.
  ISBN 978-0-13-171413-7
 1. Reading—Remedial teaching—Case studies.   2. Teachers—In-service training.
I. Title.
  LB1050.5.B513 2009
  372.43—dc22   2007052959

Printed in the United States of America

10 9 8 7 6 5 4 3 2 1   RRD-OH   09 08

Preface

*N*egotiating Literacy Learning: Exploring the Challenges and Achievements of Struggling Readers, K–6 offers teaching cases in which real teachers describe their challenges with struggling readers and explain how they help each child achieve his or her full potential. Although many of us in teacher education offer our students a variety of models (i.e., instructional videos, journal articles, field observations) on effective literacy instruction, often these examples don't reveal the decision making and problem solving that teachers go through before they find a method that is successful. The stories in this text offer the needed examples in literacy courses and professional development for exploring the learning process of teaching to negotiate the challenges of literacy learning.

Each chapter presents one case, and each case is organized to illustrate a teacher's instructional decision-making process informed by assessments, the professional literature, observation, and an ongoing reflection of practice. The chapters also provide a framework that features the teaching and learning cycle of each practitioner. Although the format is standard, each learner and teacher presents a unique story. Some teachers make greater use of the research; others place greater emphasis on observing and assessing their students. Our stories aim to tell not only *what* we did with a child but also *how* we arrived at that point. This book is an appropriate supplemental text to undergraduate and graduate courses in literacy methods, reading diagnosis and assessment, and practicum. It is also well suited for professional development and teacher study groups.

Acknowledgments

I thank the teachers and authors who agreed to share their stories and the learners who taught us so much about literacy challenges and our own teaching and learning process. I would like to thank the following advisors at Merrill for their strong support and guiding feedback: Linda Bishop, Laura Weaver, and Becky Savage. Thanks also to the reviewers of my manuscript for their helpful insights and comments: Timothy R. Blair, University of Central Florida; Nancy Bertrand, Middle Tennessee State University; Randal L. Donelson, The Ohio State University; Debbie East, Indiana University; Barbara Pettegrew, Otterbein College (Emerita); and Suzanne M. Rose, Slippery

Rock University. In addition, I am grateful to those colleagues, friends, and family who commented on drafts and answered questions: Chris Orringer, Megan Kaste, Roseann Kaste, and Gerri Mongillo. In particular, I thank my husband Jim for being very supportive of my time to "work on the book" from listening to ideas to cooking dinner, and driving me to Starbucks during an 8-hour power outage.

About the Authors

Janine Bixler, PhD in Language and Literacy Education, is an associate professor in literacy education at Mount Saint Mary College. Her case study about Eric is based on her work in a New York City public school to support a first-grade teacher in her classroom and to provide additional one-on-one support for three struggling readers in the class, while on faculty for City University of New York. Janine shared her first-grade teaching and problem solving with Eric and the other first graders with her undergraduate reading methods class, who were in need of models and opportunities to think through real examples of assessments and instructional methods addressed in the course. She has served the field of education for more than 15 years, in Georgia and New York.

Melissa Agnetti, MS in Education, is a fourth grade teacher in a widely diverse, Title 1 New York City public school. Melissa moves with each fourth-grade class to fifth grade, a practice called looping. Her study on Maria and her Reading Buddies program was written during her fourth year of teaching. Melissa continues to inspire the teachers in her school to try new ideas. Reading Buddies has had a renewed popularity since she shared her study. In addition, Melissa wrote a grant to receive her school's first Smart Board and gives professional development and PTA presentations on topics that include writing workshop, balanced literacy, technology, and differentiated instruction.

Jaime Berry, MS in Education, is an elementary classroom teacher for a New York City school, who loops with her students from second to third grade. She was in her second year of teaching when she completed her case study on teaching vocabulary with a focus on Tina. Jaime was enrolled in an alternative Master's Program in Education offered by the New York City Board of Education and the City University of New York, in response to the teacher shortage in New York City. Jaime moved to New York City, a big contrast from growing up in small-town Antlers, Oklahoma. In her pursuit to improve her teaching, she seeks ways to get her kids to become excited about reading, writing, and communicating.

Margaret Falcone, MS in Education, conducted her case study on her tutoring experience with Nikki as a master's-degree student in education.

Teaching is Margaret's second career. Her previous degree was in accounting, in which she worked as an auditor. In between careers, Margaret raised two children, volunteered at a local school to provide reading support, and served as a Girl Scout leader. Currently, Margaret is a technology cluster teacher for a K–5 New York City public school, where she teaches computer literacy and content area learning through technology.

Patricia Isoldi, MS in Education, is currently a fifth-grade teacher for a diverse, Title 1 New York City public school. She has taught in both a collaborative team teaching model with a special education teacher and in traditional classroom settings. Patty was in her fourth year of teaching when she worked with Rosa. In addition to fifth grade, she has also taught in grades 2 and 3. She serves as a grade-level leader in her school.

Kimberly Jennerich, MS in Education, is a kindergarten teacher in a Title 1 New York City public school. Her study on Tamara took place during her third year of teaching. Kimberly's classroom is designated as a model classroom for other teachers to observe. She also leads staff development in literacy and math. Outside of the classroom, Kimberly enjoys working at the Staten Island Zoo, where she runs educational programs about animals and their habitats.

Arin Marcus Rusch, MS in Education, is a sixth-grade teacher for a Title 1 New York City public middle school. At the time of her study on Juan, she was in her second year of teaching. Arin came to teaching through an alternative master's program, where she earned her master's degree while teaching in a hard-to-staff school in New York City. She is currently completing a certificate program in Educational Leadership through the Teachers College Summer Principal's Academy.

Judy Stephenson, PhD in Language and Literacy Education, is a literacy specialist for the Gwinnett County School System, in the Metropolitan Atlanta area. As a specialist, Judy provides staff development, literacy coaching, and literacy intervention for students who are struggling as readers and writers. She has more than 20 years of classroom experience and has worked with a diversity of learners, including English Language Learners and special education students, in both Canada and the United States. Donnie's classroom teacher approached Judy with her concerns about Donnie at the beginning of the school year, and together they collaborated on an intervention program that included small-group work with his teacher and after-school literacy support with Judy.

Contents

Introduction

This book was inspired by the voices of teachers like you who so often comment on a certain void in the research and professional literature: How to help the particular learners who struggle in our classrooms each day, despite our attempts to use methods of "best practice"? This book is also a response to prospective teachers who admit that they are overwhelmed when working with learners, even though they may know ways to assess them and what effective instruction looks like. Most important, this book is for all of us who believe that teaching is a profession that requires a commitment to learning from and listening to our students, regardless of the number of years we have been teaching.

Negotiating Literacy Learning: Exploring the Challenges and Achievements of Struggling Readers, K–6 features eight teachers' stories about how they engaged in the problem-solving process to meet the particular needs of their readers who struggle the most. We hope that by sharing our stories, you will learn from our own experiences as we reflected on our practice and adapted our teaching until we helped learners succeed. We also hope that you will see yourself and your students in these pages and will be inspired to share your own stories with others. We teach in a time of instituted mandates from the national level that were implemented in an effort to provide all learners an equitable education (No Child Left Behind, 2002). Although emphasis is placed on implementing literacy instruction that is scientifically based, the voices of this book remind us that no instructional approach or program is successful without the teacher negotiating and adapting instruction to the needs, interests, and background of the diverse learners she or he encounters. We hope that the stories shared about our teaching will inspire conversations and actions on how to reach all learners so they can achieve success and to prepare them to be lifelong readers, writers, and communicators.

The authors of this book are teacher-researchers who work with K–6 learners from urban and metropolitan public school systems. We represent a range of teaching experience (1–20+ years) and roles (classroom teacher, master's degree student in education, literacy specialist, and teacher educator in literacy). Some of us began our teaching calling as undergraduates, and others are career changers. In addition, each of us worked within our particular school system's interpretation of a balanced literacy curriculum (Heydon,

Hibbert, & Iannacci, 2004). Six of the authors are practicing teachers who I had the benefit of mentoring and learning from as they completed their capstone course for their master of science in education. Their stories capture the journeys they traveled as beginning teacher-researchers. Judy Stephenson (author of Chapter 3) is a colleague I met during our PhD program in language and literacy education. Judy tells her story from the perspective of a literacy specialist, an important voice to include.

Recognizing that as literacy teachers, we support our struggling learners in a variety of contexts, these stories are also told from a range of learning environments. Some of our stories resulted from working with individuals outside the classroom to provide after-school support. Others of us created contexts for small-group and individualized instruction as part of our daily classroom routines and carefully collected data on the child who challenged us the most.

Each of us first identified a literacy challenge with a struggling reader and searched the literature for best practices for instruction. Our stories share how we implemented these practices and documented our progress and adaptations as we worked to improve a particular challenging area with learners. We explored ways to motivate and be culturally responsive in our practices to improve the school literacy learning of students of diverse backgrounds (Au, 1998, 2002). Our cases reveal a wide array of experiences as we attempt to portray the challenges and uncertainties that we encountered in our day, and what we did to try to close the literacy gap. Teaching truly is learning! Our students teach us as much as we teach them, particularly when our social and cultural worlds differ from one another.

As you read each case, consider the following questions to guide your reading experience and discussions with other teacher-learners:

- Given the title of the chapter, what do you already know about the topic and the challenges that learners and teachers face at this level?
- What do you notice about the way the teacher's actions are informed by assessments, a review of the professional literature, listening to the learner, and reflection on practice?
- How have the teacher and learner in this case invited you to reflect on your own teaching and learning?

References

Au, K. H. (1998). Social constructivism and the school literacy learning of students of diverse backgrounds. *Journal of Literacy Research, 30,* 297–319.

Au, K. (2002). Multicultural factors and the effective instruction of students of diverse backgrounds. In A. E. Farstrup & S. Samuels (Eds.), *What research has to say about reading instruction* (pp. 392–413). Newark, DE: International Reading Association.

Heydon, R., Hibbert, K., & Iannacci, L. (2004). Strategies to support balanced literacy approaches in pre- and inservice teacher education. *Journal of Adolescent & Adult Literacy, 48*, 312–319.

No Child Left Behind Act of 2001, Pub. L. No. 107-110, 115 Stat. 1425 (2002).

1 | Cultivating Phonological Awareness

Helping a Kindergartner Learn About Our Spoken and Printed Language

Kimberly Jennerich, Kindergarten Teacher

"I can't do that, Ms. Jennerich!"
Kindergartner, Tamara

When Tamara first came into my kindergarten classroom she was quiet. She didn't share the excitement that other children in my room felt about learning about print. Tamara rarely raised her hand or even attempted to complete tasks. At the beginning of the year, I would give the children morning phonemic awareness activities that would review the sounds we were learning that week. All activities would be modeled first. For example, I would give them a sheet with approximately five rows, each row consisting of three pictures. Students were orally instructed to circle the picture in each row that begins with a specific sound we had worked on that week. To begin their development of alphabetic principle (Ehri, 1998)—the understanding that specific sounds are represented by particular letters—I later asked students to write the beginning letter sound of a word after I pronounced the word to them. I also modeled journal writing to encourage students' beginning writing attempts. Each day the children were given a topic to respond to in their journals. They were encouraged to draw a picture or write a simple sentence. For example: One day our topic was animals. Children were asked to think about their favorite animals and then write a sentence using their knowledge of sight-word vocabulary. Many children wrote "I like dogs.", "I like cats." and so on. The sight words were located on the word wall and in the children's sight-word folders. All of the children would attempt all of these tasks and often felt success because of the work we had done earlier, the modeling I provided, and their access to word walls. Tamara, however, did not even try. Tamara would play with her pencil, talk to other children at her table, or become occupied with her backpack. One day I asked Tamara, "Why haven't you started your work?" Tamara simply responded with a smile, "I can't do that, Ms. Jennerich!" When I asked, "Why?" Tamara just looked at me and shrugged her shoulders, offering no reason. I realized that Tamara's needs were not being met. I began to work more closely with Tamara.

The First Hurdle: Tamara Seeing Herself as a Learner

Initially I wasn't sure if Tamara had learning challenges or if she just didn't see herself as being a reader and writer. Several conversations took place with the assistant principal, guidance counselor, and Tamara's grandmother and mother about Tamara. The guidance counselor, after observing her classroom behaviors and speaking to Tamara's grandmother about her background (born prematurely, born addicted to substances, and suffered from fetal alcohol syndrome) suggested an evaluation for a learning disability. The tests did not show any signs that Tamara was learning disabled. I arranged a meeting with Tamara's family in order to begin academic intervention. I spoke with her family about the types of activities I did in the classroom and suggested ways for them to read with Tamara and involve her in some of their literacy routines at home. Not only did we need to build Tamara's literacy skills, we needed to build an interest in learning about language through sounds and texts. Tamara's grandmother offered to work with her at home. I concluded the meeting by sharing with the family how I would include Tamara in additional small-group lessons as well as find opportunities to work with her one on one.

Knowing Where to Begin

To create a plan for how I would provide additional support for Tamara in my classroom, I began with what I learned from the results of ECLAS-2, Early Childhood Literacy Assessment Skills (CTB/ McGraw-Hill, 2003) and my observations of Tamara's class performance. ECLAS-2 is an assessment tool developed for my school system to monitor a child's early literacy development from grades kindergarten to grade three. The four strands include:

- Phonemic awareness
- Phonics
- Reading and oral expression
- Listening and writing

There are several activities in each strand of the ECLAS-2. The activities I administered were to assess whether my kindergartners met benchmarks expected for our grade.

Phonemic Awareness Assessments

I first assessed Tamara on rhyme recognition. I orally gave Tamara a set of words and she had to respond yes or no to indicate whether a set rhymed. For example: *cat-goose, do my words rhyme?* Tamara's score was 3/6. The second activity was rhyme generation. During this activity Tamara had to be able to complete my riddle with a rhyming word that matched the enunciated word.

For example: *The little brown **mouse** lives in a* _____ (CTB/ McGraw-Hill, 2003). The correct answer would be any word that rhymes with *mouse* even if the answer is not logical. Tamara scored 3/6. The last activity assessed in this strand was initial consonants. The object of this activity was for Tamara to hear the beginning sound in a word. For example: I would say the word *see*, and Tamara would have to reply using the sound of */s/* only. Tamara scored 0/8.

Phonics Assessment

The phonics strand assessed letter recognition and whether she could name an appropriate sound for each letter. Tamara scored:

- Identification of uppercase letters: 2/26
- Identification of lowercase letters: 1/26
- Identification of letter sounds: 1/26

The expected benchmark for this component was to score at least 18/26 for identification of letters and 13/26 for sound identification. During these strands Tamara was frustrated and no longer wished to engage in these activities. Throughout the testing, even though it was broken up into a period of several days, Tamara would repeat, "I can't do that" or "I don't know."

Reading and Oral Expression

Next I assessed Tamara's ability to identify concepts of print. Based on the work of Marie Clay, this assessment asks a learner to share in a book-reading experience to see what the child knows about the language and concepts associated with reading (see Clay, 2005). Here, too, Tamara scored below grade-level benchmarks. She was able to tell the difference between the front of the book and back of the book. She was also able to open the book to the first page of the story, but she could not differentiate between print and pictures, demonstrate page sequencing, or show that she knew word boundaries.

Listening and Writing

For the listening and writing strand of the ECLAS-2 I read the story *Pete's Chicken* aloud to Tamara and asked her to draw a picture in response to the story. Tamara was unable to convey any meaning about the story or her picture. When I asked her, "Tell me about your picture," she responded, "It's a cat." When I asked if there was a cat in the story, Tamara replied, "Yes." *Pete's Chicken* is about a rabbit that attempts to draw a picture of a turkey, and his friends make fun of him by calling it a chicken. Tamara used the whole paper for her drawing without being able to differentiate between top and bottom when prompted. There was also no explanation for her picture "floating" in the air.

I also analyzed Tamara's writing attempts in class and assessed her writing with a rubric, which I created to document progress over time. In these writings,

I observed that she could not differentiate between the beginning of the line and the end of a line. Tamara would write in the middle or on the bottom of the page. Her formations consisted of scribble shapes with what appeared to be the beginning of correct letter writing. After each writing activity I asked Tamara if she could explain or tell me something about her picture and writing. Tamara's response was very limited: She would say, "I don't know," or she would simply shrug her shoulders and not respond.

All of these assessments showed me that Tamara had limited interest in and exposure to print and being read to, as well as limited experiences with playing with sounds in our language. Tamara would look at the other children in the room and stare at their work. Other children in the class began to notice that Tamara was unable to complete her work. I heard one child in our classroom say to Tamara, "You don't know what you're doing—let me help you."

 ## Literacy Challenges: Learner and Teacher

I knew that Tamara was lacking many of the skills that other children in my class had. But first I had to find something that motivated her to want to learn about language and to engage in reading and writing activities. Eventually I found something to begin to pique her interest. At the same time that I was trying to figure out Tamara, I was being trained with the other teachers in my building in the Wilson Fundations program (Wilson Fundations, 2002). Fundations is a program intended to complement a teacher's reading curriculum to develop phonological awareness, phonics, and early spelling. One of the components of Fundations involves the use of a mother and baby owl puppet named Mama Echo and Baby Echo. When I introduced the two owls to the class, Tamara was extremely excited and wanted to touch and interact with them. After observing Tamara's response to these puppets, I decided to use puppetry as a way to build Tamara's interest and literacy skills. One activity I used in the classroom incorporated our classroom letter puppets. With each puppet, I taught students a song that emphasized the letter and its sounds. The songs included words that began with the featured letter. One song that Tamara enjoyed for the letter M puppet is shown here.

> Monkey see monkey do
>
> Come see monkey in the zoo
>
> If you make a face he might make one too
>
> Monkeys love to mimic you*

*From ABC SING-ALONG FLIP CHART AND TAPE by Teddy Slater. Copyright © 2000 by Teddy Slater. Reprinted by permission of Scholastic Inc.

Because of Tamara's positive response to the owl puppets, I began to use more songs and puppetry. The songs were short enough for Tamara to remember and easy enough to learn quickly. These songs gave her an opportunity to develop her phonological awareness of the different sounds in our language.

During our individual sessions together, we used the letter puppets to develop her limited alphabet recognition. Using the puppets and the alphabet song (*ABCDEFG, HIJKLMNOP, QRS, TUV, WX, YZ, now I know my ABC's—next time won't you sing with me*?) Tamara and I would touch each letter puppet while singing. This enabled her to visually see and name the letter puppets to begin learning the letter symbols. Tamara was aware that for every letter she sang she would move her hand across the letter. She was proud of herself that she was able to do this. During the third session doing this activity Tamara exclaimed "I can do this, this is easy!" After repeating the same activity for the fourth time I decided to make the activity more difficult. During our next session I presented Tamara with three puppets in alphabetical order, ABC. I asked her to identify the names of the letters. She replied, "I don't know the names of those letters." I reassured and encouraged her to sing the alphabet song, but I stopped her at C. I then asked her "Do you know why I stopped you at C?" She replied, "No." I asked her to sing the song again and touch the puppets while singing the song just like we have done previously. I asked her if she noticed anything similar. Tamara said, "Ms. Jennerich, I don't know my letters." I repeated the same directions, "Sing the alphabet song slowly and touch the puppets." I stopped her at "C" once again. I then told her that when she sang the song and touched the puppets, she was touching a different letter that is part of the song. I displayed all twenty-six puppets, and we sang and touched all puppets together. I then took away all puppets except for A, B, and C. I asked Tamara to sing again and stopped her at "C." "Why did I stop you at the letter C?" Tamara responded, "Because I only have ABC!" Although this more difficult lesson exhausted both of us, success was achieved. I continued in exactly the same pattern for future sessions to use as a review of letters taught in class. Tamara now showed interest and self-confidence as she began to make the connection between the song and different letter names and the actual letters. Tamara even began to participate during whole class discussions. It was now time to move ahead and begin activities from the new Fundations program (Wilson Fundations, 2002).

Challenges with Explicit Instruction

One part of the Fundations program is a "skill and drill" segment of each letter (Wilson Fundations, 2002). This segment includes learning letters and sounds through large sound cards. Each card contains a letter and a keyword picture representing the word with that sound. For example:

Aa (picture of apple), Bb (picture of bat), Cc (picture of cat)

The owl puppet mentioned earlier, Mama Echo, was used to introduce the sound card by asking if anyone knows the letter on the card. If the children did not recognize the letter, I would say the letter name. I would then ask the children whether anyone knew the picture. If the children were unfamiliar with the picture, I would say the name of the picture, emphasizing the beginning sound. The final step is to have children "echo." The teacher's job is to have Mama Echo perched on her arm as if it was a branch, then say the letter, keyword, and sound.

During whole-class instruction, Tamara seemed fascinated with the puppet. It was now the children's turn to actively participate using the puppet, Baby Echo. For children to be able to participate with Baby Echo, small sound cards are placed on the chalkboard permanently *without* the keyword picture as the letters are introduced. The children's job was to choose a letter and from memory say the letter, keyword and sound, and then proceed to fly Baby Echo above for students to repeat. At first Tamara was shy but tried with assistance. "*T*, top." The other students were able to help her out with the beginning sound /t/. By the time I introduced the second set of letters, increasing each week by two new letters, Tamara was an active participant. I thought Tamara was finally making progress in letter sound relationships. After all sounds were introduced, I assessed Tamara in letter sound recognition. To my disappointment, Tamara was only able to recite the segments by rote; she was unable to make any connections between letters and sounds beyond the cards. For example, I would ask, "What is the sound of *k*?" Tamara would respond "*k, kite* /k/." Tamara would reply in this manner for all letters, not being able to differentiate between letter, sound, and keyword or picture. Nor could she identify sounds or letters with anything beyond the cards. Tamara had only memorized the cards. Even after I gave Tamara the large sound card to assist her, she was still only able to repeat by rote, without isolating or distinguishing the difference between a letter, sound, and word.

 ## Addressing the Challenge

I knew I had to make these sessions with Tamara more meaningful so that she would be able to understand how our language works. Tamara had a terrific memory but was still not making the connection. I needed to build on her spoken language abilities to create literacy activities that were purposeful for Tamara. I decided to engage her in phonemic awareness games that helped her to identify and manipulate sounds (Yopp & Yopp, 2000). Because of Tamara's limited print knowledge, I also aimed to embed phonemic awareness instruction in meaningful reading and writing activities (Richgels, Poremba & McGee, 1996).

Phonemic Awareness Games

We played word games that helped her to match and isolate sounds in words by exploring names that she knew. For example I pronounced the /t/ sound and told Tamara I was thinking of someone whose name started with the sound of /t/. "Tamara, what letter begins with /t/?" She replied, "*T*." I then asked her, "What sound does your name begin with?" She replied "/t/ like in *t*, top /t/." Tamara and I did this game for several sessions using the names of her friends in the classroom. Eventually she began to isolate sounds with less reliance on reciting all the information from the cards. Another variation of the name game was to take away the initial sound of a given name and see if she could guess the person with part of that name. For example: *Shaniqua* becomes *aniqua*. Then I'd ask her for the missing sound /sh/ (Lock, Flett, & Conderman, 2002).

The second game we played in order to make meaningful connections was placing daily objects that are easily recognized in a paper bag. Tamara was then instructed to close her eyes and choose an item from the bag. Once she had the item in her hand, she would have to name the item and the sound it began with. All items in the bag pertained to one of the letters previously taught that week. For example, I placed markers, a monkey, and a milk carton in a paper bag. I limited the bag to three objects so that Tamara would not feel overwhelmed. To my surprise, not only was Tamara successful in giving the sound and letter, she also began looking around our classroom to find objects that began with the /m/ sound. Tamara was on her way to making connections! I also did this activity several times using different beginning sounds in one bag. Tamara was able to grasp all letter sounds in this manner without difficulty.

Learning Letters and Their Sounds

We played a puzzle game in which children stood in two lines facing one another. One line had all picture puzzle pieces, the other line had the letter puzzle piece. The object of the game was to match their piece to the adjoining piece. All puzzle pieces corresponded to our Fundations sound cards (Wilson Fundations, 2002). For example: Tamara was holding the puzzle piece with a picture of a cat on it. Tamara had to look at all the letters standing across from her and decide which was the beginning sound and letter. At first she was unable to decide and quickly responded, "I don't know." I encouraged her to take her time and told her, "You know the answer. Look at all the letters and decide which begins with *cat*." Tamara continued looking, so I asked her, "What sound does *cat* begin with?" She quickly responded, "/k/." Tamara then looked at me and said "*Kite* also begins with /k/." I told her she was correct. I asked her, "Which two letters have the /k/ sound?" She responded "K and *C*." I then urged her to think back to when she first saw the picture of the cat on the large sound card. She immediately responded "C!" and matched her puzzle piece.

I also exposed Tamara and other children to other contexts to learn their letter names and corresponding sounds. Alphabet Bingo (Trend Enterprises, 2002) is played by the facilitator calling out letter names for the children to visually recognize. Sound Bingo is played by the facilitator calling out letter sounds, and then the children must place a counter on the corresponding letter in order to match the correct sound. Over time, Tamara found Alphabet Bingo easy. Tamara would say the letter called and then say a word that began with the same letter. At first, during Sound Bingo she seemed frustrated; she would just stare at the letter board. After coaxing, Tamara began repeating the sound and then saying a word that began with the same letter, usually a word from our Fundations sound card. Each day she was becoming more confident in her identification of letters and sounds. I decided to help her make use of the word wall in our room as a tool for making connections. This would later help her with her sight word recognition, too.

Making Connections to the Word Wall

Over time, Tamara was able to make the connection that words are made of sounds and sounds are represented by different letters. Occasionally she would get stuck in attaching the letter to the correct sound. During a consonant game, I helped Tamara make use of the classroom word wall when she was stuck.

J: What are you thinking about?

T: I'm trying to think.

J: About what?

T: Letters, Ms. Jennerich!

J: What about letters?

T: The letter that begins with *bear*.

J: What do you know about the letter that begins with *bear*?

T: I know it has the same letter as *ball*.

J: Do you mean sound?

T: Yes.

J: What sound do you hear first in *bear* and *ball*?

T: /b/

J: Do you know the letter?

T: No.

J: Where can you find a picture of a bear or a ball?

T: In the classroom?

J: Yes. Where in the classroom can you find a picture of a bear or ball?

T: The wall.

J: What wall?

T: (She points but is unable to verbalize "word wall.")

J: Point to the picture of the ball on the word wall. (Tamara points.) What letter does *ball* begin with?

T: *b*

Tamara continued to use the word wall as a source to assist her in letter-sound relationships while playing this game. I also noticed Tamara using the word wall and her sight-word folder during journal writing. This helped Tamara to attempt to write sentences. Tamara was making great progress.

Rebus Sentences

Tamara began to develop an understanding of how letters form words, which contain meaning. We next moved on to rebus sentences (Lakeshore, 2003) to help Tamara decode and encode words in simple sentences. The rebus sentences incorporate learned sight words with pictures to represent unknown words: for example, *I saw a* (picture of a cow). This activity also helped her to reinforce the sight words we addressed in class and to get her ready to read level "A" books. Rebus sentences became a favorite activity for Tamara. She liked being able to use pictures in her created sentences and eventually drew her own pictures to represent words she did not know by sight or couldn't spell phonetically. Tamara took picture cards that she enjoyed working with and began to point to sight words that she knew. When she became frustrated or bored she would say, "Let's make our own sentences." Tamara would draw a picture on an index card and use it in her sentence. For example: Tamara drew a picture of a rabbit, then wrote the words *I* and *like* on separate index cards. Tamara was then instructed to place the words in order to create her sentence, "I like (picture of a rabbit)." Sometimes she would get too comfortable with the same sight words and needed encouragement to try others. For example, when she drew a picture of her mother, I asked her, "What would you like to write about your mom?" She replied, "My mom is fun." I instructed her to use the words from the word wall to help her. Tamara was able to write *My* and place the picture of her mother next to *My*. She then began to sound out her words and wrote the words on index cards using inventive spelling. I was extremely proud of Tamara that she was using her developing phoneme knowledge to attempt new words. Her sentence looked like this: "My (picture of her mom) iz f" I asked, her if she "heard any other sounds in *fun*" focusing on the middle and ending sounds. To her surprise she heard /n/. Tamara then went back to her index card and wrote the letter *n* next to *f*. Tamara's inventive spelling for *fun* was "fn."

Tamara began to know more sight words and to have a greater understanding of print concepts. By midyear she was able to read an A-level book by matching spoken words to print. An A-level book titled *I Like* (Pinnell, 2000) has repetitive phrases such as "I like to eat. I like to sleep." The sight words on each page remain the same; only the picture clues with corresponding words change. This support gave Tamara greater confidence and interest and more opportunities to practice words. Tamara changed from an uninterested reader to an enthusiastic reader.

Fitting Instruction to Meet the Needs of Tamara

Working with Tamara taught me so much about early literacy instruction. Often we jump to conclusions about why a learner is not performing well. Tamara came to us with a difficult history. In her case, it was not so much any physical effects that caused the delay, but a need to invite Tamara into the literacy club (Smith, 1985) where she, too, valued herself as a reader and writer.

I was successful with Tamara because I first looked for something that interested her. In the beginning I was focused on what she wasn't accomplishing in my room. When I looked to see what she did like, I was able to use that interest to introduce opportunities to think about the spoken and written word. In Tamara's case, the puppets amused and interested her, so I extended the Fundations' owl puppet idea to introducing her to letter puppets. I also incorporated games that helped her to play with language using names and the everyday words that were important to Tamara.

I also learned about the importance of fitting explicit instruction and practice to meet her needs. Although the letter cards seemed to help Tamara learn about letters and sounds, I soon found out that she began to depend too much on these and was not able to apply what she was learning to other contexts. The games and other word activities helped with this. I also learned that sometimes it took her a while to catch on to learning a new concept. I made time to work with her one-on-one: modeled reading, writing, and playing with words; and gave her a comfortable environment so that she would be more expressive about what she did and didn't understand.

By late spring Tamara still scored below grade level but showed much improvement. In letter sound recognition she scored 24/26, up from 2/26. In sound recognition she scored 21/26, up from 1/26. This time she was able to differentiate between letter sounds without doing rote memorization. When I reassessed her in isolating initial sounds she scored 5/8, compared to 0/8.

When I look at Tamara now, I see a little girl who is not afraid to take risks and always smiles. When I work together with Tamara, she looks at me, smiles, and laughs after writing and reading her own sentence. When I ask her, "What is so funny?" she replies, "I can write a sentence!"

References

Clay, M. M. (2005). *An observation survey of early literacy achievement* (2nd ed.). Portsmouth, NH: Heinemann.

CTB/McGraw-Hill. (2003). *ECLAS*. Developed and published under contract with the New York City Department of Education. Monterey, CA: McGraw-Hill.

Ehri, L. C. (1998). Grapheme-phoneme knowledge is essential for learning to read words in English. In J. L. Metsala & Ehri, L. C. (Eds.), *Word recognition in beginning literacy* (pp. 3–40). Mahwah, NJ: Erlbaum.

Fountas, I. C. & Pinnell, G. S. (1998). *Word matters*. Portsmouth, NH: Heinemann.

Lakeshore. (2003). *Sight word sentence builder kit*. Carson, CA: Lakeshore.

Lock, R. H., Flett, A., & Conderman, G. (2002). Promote phonemic awareness. *Intervention in School and Clinic, 37*, 242–245.

Pinnell, G. S. (2000). *I like*. New York: Scholastic.

Richgels, D. J., Poremba, K. J., & McGee, L. M. (1996). Kindergarteners talk about print: Phonemic awareness in meaningful context. *The Reading Teacher, 49*, 632–642.

Schaffer, F. (1997). *Learning games initial consonant game*. Torrance, CA: Schaffer Publications.

Slater, T. (2000). *ABC sing-along flip chart & tape*. New York: Scholastic.

Smith, F. (1985). *Reading without nonsense* (2nd ed.). New York: Teachers College.

Trend Enterprises. (2002). *Alphabet bingo*. St. Paul, MN: Trend Enterprises.

Wilson Fundations. (2002). *Fundations*. Millbury, MA: Wilson Language Training Corporation.

Yopp, K. K. & Yopp, R. H. (2000). Supporting phonemic awareness development in the classroom. *The Reading Teacher, 54*, 130–143.

2 | Developing Reading and Writing Fluency

Building a Student's Automatic Vocabulary Through
Repeated Readings and Language Experience Approach

Janine Bixler, Teacher Educator

"I can't read a book!"
First Grader, Eric

When I met Eric, he wanted me to believe that he was a good reader and he tried to convince me that he could read well. He really wanted to read like other first graders, but believed that he couldn't and was frustrated. During our first session together, I asked Eric, "Do you think you are a good reader?" Eric responded, "Yes!" But when I asked "Why? What makes you a good reader?", he shrugged and said indifferently, "I don't know."

When I asked Eric to read something for me, he tried to alter the task. I chose a passage-length story with a simple picture to determine his instructional reading level. I began by pointing out the drawing of the characters in the story and asked him to make predictions about the story through the picture. He interrupted with, "Oh, let me color it in. I should have brought my crayons." He then proceeded to tell me each color that he would use for the two children and dog in the picture. Later, I asked him to sort a pile of picture books so that I could learn about what he would be interested in reading. Eric did not look through any of the books, like most children. Instead he quickly put every book in the "Yes" pile, ignoring the place for "no" and "maybe" piles.

It wasn't until our third session together that Eric felt comfortable to tell me what he really believed. On that day, I showed him a leveled book that I knew he could read with my support, but even before I had a chance to introduce the book to him, Eric looked directly into my eyes and interrupted, "I can't read a book!"

The First Hurdle: Eric Seeing Himself as a Reader

Eric was convinced that he couldn't learn to read. He knew that his mother was concerned that he couldn't read. My phone conversations with her and her talks with the assistant principal of the school made it clear that Eric knew that she, too, felt that there was something wrong. I knew from my reading interview with Eric that he noticed other first graders reading books that he couldn't. He spoke highly of his classmate, Lorenzo, who could read a whole page to the class without mistakes. In the classroom, I observed that Eric avoided opportunities that would expose what he believed he couldn't do. He made every effort to escape reading out loud. One time when he was asked to read, he claimed that his throat hurt too much. He also lost interest in tracking print when others read. To compensate for falling behind, Eric would copy his classmate's work, act silly to make other's laugh, or write down words that he knew how to spell, regardless of the activity.

From the time we spent together, it was clear to me that Eric really wanted to learn how to read but was afraid that he was not capable. My challenge would be to help Eric see himself as a reader.

 ## Knowing Where to Begin

During the next 5-month period, I worked both one-on-one with Eric and in his classroom with his teacher. Before I determined where to begin with instruction, I observed Eric's behaviors in class and recorded them. Then, I administered a variety of assessment tools. These included:

- Informal Reading Inventory (IRI; Johns, 1997)
- Burke Reading Interview (Goodman, Watson, & Burke, 1987)
- Phonemic Segmentation (Yopp, 1995)
- Eric's writing
- Eric's oral reading from a self-selected book

Results from the Informal Reading Inventory

From the word list and oral reading passage at the pre-primer level of the IRI, I learned that Eric knew a few words by sight. He was not able to read the passage successfully. His initial strategy was to guess at a word based on the initial letter, or occasionally use a similar word (for example, *look* for *took*) that he had already learned, regardless if it made sense in the text. For example, he read the title *Walk in the Fall* as "With in the Farm." Below is the running record I took on his reading of the passage. Although he began attempting to read the passage, he quickly changed to locating words that he already knew by sight. He wanted to show me what he could read and avoid what he could not read.

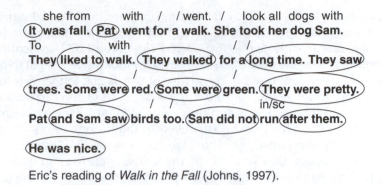

Eric's reading of *Walk in the Fall* (Johns, 1997).

Eric scored at the frustrational level for this passage and was unable to answer any comprehension questions regarding the passage. The Informal Reading Inventory showed me that although Eric did recognize some words automatically by sight, he did not know enough words, employed limited cue system strategies, and did not read for the purpose of making meaning. To look at this further, I assessed him with the Burke Reading Interview.

Information from the Burke Reading Interview

The Burke Reading Interview is a tool that assists teachers in finding out what strategies a reader uses and how they view reading (Goodman, Watson, & Burke, 1987). Eric claimed that he asked for help when he came to a word that he didn't know or "sounded it out." However, he rarely attempted to use this strategy when asked to read. As noted earlier, when I asked if he was a good reader, he asserted, "Yes," but couldn't say what made him a good reader. He identified his classmate Lorenzo as being a good reader because "he knows a lot of the work we do" and "He can read all the words on a page." He also couldn't explain how his teacher would help a learner with an unknown word other than tell the learner the word or to "sound it out."

As Eric had shown in his performance on the Informal Reading Inventory, Eric believed that reading required identifying words. The Burke Reading Interview showed that he was aware of the strategy of sounding out words, although it didn't appear to be a strategy that he used well. This told me that I needed to make Eric aware of what it meant to decode or "sound out" words and to help him learn more words to increase his automatic vocabulary. Most important, I needed to help Eric see that we read to make meaning of an author's message.

Phoneme Segmentation Assessment

Because of Eric's limited performance on the IRI (Johns, 1997), I decided to assess his phonemic awareness with the Test for Assessing Phonemic Awareness in Young Children (Yopp, 1995). This test, presented as a word game, asks a learner to segment a spoken word into its individual phonemes/sounds: For example, *wave* has three phonemes, /w/ /ā/ /v/. Eric scored 12/22, indicating that he had emerging phonemic awareness. However, in looking at his partially correct responses, it was evident that his knowledge of words and letters was interfering with his ability to focus only on the sounds. In eight of the responses, he segmented the word into its onsets and rimes, not each individual phoneme/sound, as in the word *th-at*. This may be attributed to the lessons in his classroom on word families. When returning to those words, I responded, *"th-at* is one way to break the word apart. Can you tell me the sounds you hear in /at/?" Eric was able to break down the rime further into /ā/ and /t/, and for six of the other eight words. The two words that confused him most were the two words he knew how to spell, *dog* and *no*. When segmenting *dog*, he responded /d/ /ĕ/ /j/, as if picturing the letters and trying to remember the sounds he has learned for those letters, rather than thinking about the sounds in that word. Likewise, for no he said, /n/ /ĕ/. Again he said the same sound for *o* in both words, even though /o/ in dog is a short vowel sound and /o/ in no is a long vowel sound.

Eric's Writing Sample

I also asked Eric to write something to me. He wrote his address, again drawing on what he knew he could do. I encouraged him to write me something about himself. After much hesitation, he finally wrote: *Eric likes to play with my pet*. He read his sentence, however, as, "Eric likes to play with his pet." His written text was based on those words he knew how to spell. I brought to his attention the fact that *my* did not say *his*. Although he asked me to help him spell the word *his*, I encouraged him to try on his own. He erased *my* and wrote *hed* for "his." As a writer, too, Eric was not focusing so much on communicating a message as he was to write something he could spell conventionally. This showed me that he was aware that words have a standard spelling.

Eric's Self-Selected Reading Sample

I also asked Eric to look through a pile of picture books and tell me which books he would like to read. When he saw the book *Green Eggs and Ham* (Seuss, 1960), Eric told me that he knew how to read "Sam I am," so I chose this book also to assess Eric's oral reading ability. Eric read half of the book quickly, but only because he was reading memorized phrases, and not always accurately. For example, Eric read, *Would you eat them in a box?* as "Would you could you with a box?"

Although this reading was memorized, and not accurate, Eric was familiar enough with this book to sound more like a reader and to recite the story, which he had heard many times. This was in contrast to his attempt to get through the Informal Reading Inventory passage by sporadically pointing at and identifying individual words that he could recognize by sight. It showed me that he could perform like a reader, after hearing a book read to him often enough to memorize the story.

 ## Literacy Challenges: Learner and Teacher

My assessment of Eric told me that he understood that spoken words were represented in a specific way in print. He was also aware of the sounds represented in words, yet he had little knowledge of matching the sounds to the letters, which affected both his ability to read and write fluently and his ability to make meaning from text when reading. Armed with this information, I designed our initial sessions (as well as the class sessions with his teacher) to include word study lessons that would help Eric learn words with regular and high utility patterns.

Engaging Eric in Making Words Activity

One such activity, as shown below, was "Making Words" (Cunningham, 1999). In this activity, students are given scrambled letters of a selected word and are guided to spell many smaller words. The big word is selected by the particular phonemes and rimes that a tutor or teacher wants students to study. As students are guided to spell words, they learn how words change when letters are added or switched. Later the spelled words are sorted according the common rimes they share.

Making Words for SPLASH

Words to spell: Al, pal, lap, Sal, sap, has, ash, sash, lash, pass, pals, laps, slap, slaps, slash, splash

Word sorts: rimes -al, -ap, -ash,

Example of beginning of Making Words for splash:

- Make the two letter name **Al**. Remember that a name begins with a capital letter.
- Add one letter to make the word **pal**
- Switch two of the letters to change **pal** to **lap**

From Cunningham, 1999.

As with the other two children whom I worked with individually from that class, I began by introducing word patterns in my session with Eric so that he and the other two students would feel success when I introduced the same words and patterns in their classroom. Although the other two students, who were second language learners, did very well when they had their second try in the classroom,

Eric struggled as much as he did when I introduced the patterns to him the first time. Given the clue "Spell the three-letter name Sal," he'd often choose the wrong letters (*s,h,l*), or place the letters in the incorrect order (*sla*). Eric also had difficulty with sorting words by their common rime (*ap, ash* words) and reading the word families when given the words together. Often Eric would become off-task when he realized that he wasn't able to get the word "right." I decided I needed to add another dimension to this activity to help Eric be more successful.

Using Elkonin Boxes to Extend Word Study Help

In a subsequent word study session, I tried to provide Eric more time doing word study with the same word families. When I added the use of Elkonin boxes (Clay, 1986), Eric could write the words, which let him see the letters that form each phoneme and how each phoneme or sound is represented in a word. For example, the word *pal* has three phonemes represented by three letters, *p*, *a*, *l*, and the word *lash* also has three phonemes/sounds, because the /*sh*/ sound is represented by the combined letters *s* and *h*.

Example of Elkonin Boxes with Making Words pal, lash

| p | a | l |

| l | a | sh |

As Eric read each word I had him slide a penny along the word so that he could see how the sounds and order of letters corresponded. The other students were progressing well with these activities, but Eric showed little growth. He began to be frustrated, and I was spending more and more time trying to keep him focused. Because the time that Eric was spending on word study activities showed little progress, he seemed to be more convinced he was never going to be a reader. I needed to show Eric that he could read texts now to build his confidence before he gave up completely.

 ## Addressing the Challenge

I decided that we would need to build Eric's automatic vocabulary in another way. I looked over the data from our sessions. Eric did know some words by sight as whole words and consistently identified these words correctly. I decided to make word study a secondary focus and provide repeated exposure to words in predictable texts, and find out what words were important for him to learn how to read. I decided to tap into Eric's strong verbal skills to build his reading vocabulary. I also wanted him to learn to apply his ability to consider what makes sense (semantic cues) when he read. I wanted him to read for meaning, not just pronounce words, so I chose books in his areas of interest, and we composed texts about him.

Using Leveled Texts and Repeated Readings

Many leveled books contain predictable texts and repetitive language, so I began using some with Eric that were on topics that were familiar and interesting to him. We did repeated readings (Samuels, 1997) of these texts until he could read independently (98% of the passage accurately). In repeated readings a student reads the same text more than once, with less support each time until the learner is able to read the text quickly and fluidly. In these sessions I wanted to build Eric's automatic vocabulary and use of strategic reading, secondarily attending to word study and phonics in the classroom. The day I brought his first leveled book to our session, I assured him that I was confident that he could read *this* book. I told him the title of the book, *My Dog Willy* (Peters, 1995), and we did a picture walk to predict what the text would be about. To begin our book discussion I told Eric that this was a story about a boy's pet dog. I told him that I picked this book because I remembered that he had a pet turtle. Then I guided him through a picture walk to verbally tell me what he thought was happening in the story by describing what he saw in the illustrations on each page. This built his confidence because he knew how to make meaning of the pictures. Sometimes I solicited particular vocabulary words that I thought would be tricky for him while reading. For example, when he commented that the boy and Willie were eating apples, I asked what meal did he think they were eating, since we saw on the previous page that the boy just woke up in his bed.

Eric found the first reading of this text difficult, but unlike previous readings, he was able to use the repetitive language and picture clues to decode the text.

```
     /   /   T     /   / sleep /   /   /   /    room
My dog Willy likes to wake me up in the morning.
  /   /     /   /    /  /    apples
My dog Willy likes to eat breakfast.
  /   /   /   /    /   / T   /   / T    T
My dog Willy likes to say hello to our neighbors.
                        run
  /   /    /     /  / look /   /   /
My dog Willy likes to ride in the car.
  /   /    /     /   /  /   / T     /   /   /
My dog Willy likes to go shopping at the store.
  /   /   /    /   /   /   /
My dog Willy likes to play ball.
                         wet himself
  /   /    /    /    /   /   / ball
My dog Willy likes to take a bath
  /   /   /   /    /    / T    T    T
And my dog Willy loves to make new friends.
```

Erics first reading of *My Dog Willy*. From *"My Dog Willy"* by Catherine Peters from GUIDED READING, Collection 1 in HOUGHTON MIFFLIN READING: INVITATIONS TO LITERACY by J. David Cooper and John J. Pikulski, et al. Copyright © 1995 by Houghton Mifflin Company. Reprinted by permission of Houghton Mifflin Company. All rights reserved.

Eric read this text with 83% accuracy, which indicated that it was challenging for him. He made use of the pictures to decode the text. For example, instead of *breakfast* he said "apples," noting the apples in the picture. He made some attempts to use the first letter of the word to guess the unknown word, as when he attempted "run" for *ride* and "bath" for *ball*. In the case of "bath" for *ball*, he recognized that this didn't make sense, so made the second attempt "wet himself" to fit the book's illustration. What was most successful about this reading was that he didn't believe that he could read the whole book, but he did. I knew that this was a proud accomplishment when I spoke to his mother that evening. It was the first thing that Eric told her when he arrived home from school.

Developing Reading Cues and Strategies. I supported Eric's book reading by encouraging him to use different reading cues. For example, as he read I prompted him by asking questions and then modeled out loud what readers say when they come to an unknown word. I talked to Eric about the semantic language of text when Eric read the text phrase *wakes me up in the morning* as "sleep me up in the morning." I repeated the phrase and asked him if that made sense to him. Then, when he said "in the room" for *in the morning*, I acknowledged that *room* was a guess that made sense, but to look more carefully at the word, which began with an /m/.

Multiple Readings. Eric read *My Dog Willy* four times and improved in accuracy each time. His third attempt, 3 weeks after his first reading, is shown here.

Eric's third reading was 95% accurate. In this reading, he was able to self-correct three times without assistance. He was able to get the word ride with my prompts—"Look at that word again, could that be *drive*? Can Willy *drive* a car?" I noted that he continued to have difficulty with "our" and "neighbors" and developed other context sentences for these words. We composed sentences about which first-grade class was his class's *neighbors* in the hall and who his *neighbors* were in the apartment building where he lived. We wrote the sentences from the perspective of his class and his family so that we also used the word *our*.

Over time, Eric's readings showed that he used the picture cues to help him, but he also began paying more attention to the visual aspects of words and whether the sentence made sense. For example, in one line of text he used the picture to substitute the word *instruments*, then guessed "noise" but said it as "moise" to fit the first letter, before finally getting the word *music*.

> *music*
>
> *moise*
>
> *instruments*
>
> *We like to make music.**

*From "Friends" by Catherine Peters from GUIDED READING. Collection 1 in HOUGHTON MIFFLIN READING: INVITATIONS TO LITERACY by J. David Cooper and John J. Pikulski, et al. Copyright © 1995 by Houghton Mifflin Company. Reprinted by permission of Houghton Mifflin Company. All rights reserved.

My Dog Willy (3ʳᵈ repeated reading)

/   /   /   /   /   /   /   /   //   /   /

My dog Willy likes to wake me up in the morning.

b— breakfast! sc

/   /   /   /   /   / milk

My dog Willy likes to eat breakfast.

your /T

/   /   /   /   /   /   /   / the next door/T

My dog Willy likes to say hello to our neighbors.

TTA / ride

/   /   /   /   / drive / /   /

My dog Willy likes to ride in the car.

/   /   /   /   //   /   /   /   /

My dog Willy likes to go shopping at the store.

/   /   /   /   //   /   /

My dog Willy likes to play ball.

sc

/   /   /   / / make / /

My dog Willy likes to take a bath

sc

/   /   /   / has /   /   /   /

And my dog Willy loves to make new friends.

Eric's third repeated reading of *My Dog Willy*.

I continued to give Eric more leveled books, with increased difficulty, and to revisit these texts through repeated readings. Eric improved each time, with his third attempts reaching at least 95% accuracy. I worried that he would tire of rereading books, but this was not the case. Eric could see the improvement he made by revisiting the books. I reinforced this by showing him graphs of his repeated readings. Just a month into our sessions of focusing on repeated readings, I saw a big change in his motivation and enthusiasm for reading. When beginning his first reading of the new book *Friends*, Eric giggled with satisfaction because he had just read the first two pages without hesitation. After reading two-thirds of the book, he exulted, "How much better can I read!—I want to read books that have only words on the page!"

The Language Experience Approach

In addition to repeated readings, we also used the Language Experience Approach (LEA) (Dorr, 2006; Novick, 2000) to write texts that Eric would eventually master reading. These texts were based on his interests and included vocabulary that was important to him. In addition, it gave me an opportunity to model writing and for Eric to see his ideas as written text. After reading a book, I would suggest that we write our own story, based on a similar topic. As Eric dictated his ideas out loud, I recorded them on paper in front of him.

Building on Interest and Repeated Reading Experiences. The first LEA story we wrote was "Matt the Turtle," after reading the book *My Dog Willy*. We also wrote "Cousins" which was Eric's inspiration after reading the text *Friends* (Peters, 1995). Below is the text for "Cousins." This text referenced his turtle from the first story. He also chose to include the words *castle* and *build* in his story, which were words that he had trouble with in his instructional-level book, *Friends*. I let Eric share the pen when he was comfortable writing parts of the story.

> My cousin Ernese likes to play with my turtle and me. We like to build castles and forts. We like to play in the snow. We also like to play football. Ernese and I are six years old!

Circumventing a Dependence on Memorization. We revisited the LEA texts to do repeated readings. Because I had established a rapport with his mother, I also sent home copies of his LEA stories and encouraged him to read the stories to as many people available (even Matt, his turtle). As he became comfortable with the texts, I wondered if he was relying more on memorization and would not recognize these words in new contexts. So, as he became comfortable reading texts, I placed sentences on colored sentence strips and cut them up for him to reassemble and read. By the third and fourth repeated readings, he was able to assemble and read these texts with at least 97% accuracy. Other times we took words and made new contexts for them, as in the previous example with the words *our* and *neighbors*.

Building Writing Fluency

Last, to encourage his own writing fluency, Eric wrote in a journal. As indicated in the beginning, Eric was uncomfortable taking risks to spell words inventively and would often limit his message based on what he knew he could write. On most occasions, he would not write anything meaningful because he knew that he didn't know how to spell the words he wanted to use. My challenge was to help Eric see writing as meaningful communication and not torture. Eric knew that invented spelling attempts were encouraged, but because of his limited knowledge of phonics, he was turned off by "Just try to do it the best you can."

To encourage more risk taking, and to recognize his interest in spelling words conventionally, I made Eric a personal word wall on a sheet of paper to record the spellings of challenging words. This also included words that I noted he had repeatedly had difficulty recognizing, such as *our* and *neighbors*. During a later session he wanted to write about his field trip to the crayon factory. Eric asked me to record the words *colored, crayons, watched, factory,* and *Queens.* The other words he spelled conventionally or was willing to attempt himself.

> I padite a cat. I used blue, green, red, yellow and orange. I colored a kiten. I watched the man make crayons. The crayon factory is in Queens.

A	B	C colored crayons	D
E	F factory	G	H
I	J	K	L
M	N neighbor	O our	P
Q Queens	R	S	T
U	V	W watched	X
Y	Z		

Eric, the Risk Taker. Eric began to consider what he wanted to say rather than what he could write conventionally. He began to take risks and pay attention to words. Print used to overwhelm him, but now he was beginning to see how our language worked. He even began to attempt to spell words inventively, as in the word *padite* for painted. He was starting to show evidence that he was representing sounds in words appropriately. As he became more confident, I wondered how I could get him to write more independently. This would be key for the classroom when the teacher could not sit with him to give him spellings of the words he wanted to spell all of the time. In later writing tasks, I told Eric to attempt all spellings first and underline the word when he thought it wasn't spelled correctly. That way he could get help or go back to these words when he had finished putting all of his ideas down. He liked this idea. It allowed him to show others that he knew his spelling attempt was not right and seemed to allow him to worry less about spelling and more about what he wanted to say.

Fitting Instruction to Meet the Needs of the Child

Eric's challenges reminded me that best practices are not best for all children. Because word study and phonics did not come easily for Eric, he grew very frustrated that reading wasn't coming as easily to him as it was for many of his first-grade peers. It was important that I emphasize, the goal of instruction (Au, 1998) for Eric: to provide him with a sense of ownership in our lessons. Eric desperately wanted to be able to read a book. He needed to see that there was a way to understand what readers do and to have access to these processes. Engaging Eric in repeated reading of texts and language experience stories tapped into his strengths—sense meaning-making and the memorization of whole words. Using these strategies to design instruction helped Eric to develop his vocabulary more quickly than if I had tried to teach him word families and phonics by analogy alone. Eric needed to succeed in reading whole books and in writing to communicate real messages. He needed to learn words that interested him. Eventually his confidence and larger automatic vocabulary supported him in being more successful in later phonics/word study lessons.

Instructional Materials Relevant to Eric's Interests

To feed Eric's interest and access his prior knowledge, the instructional materials I chose to use were on topics that he could relate to or chose himself, as in the case of his language experience stories. One of the first challenging books that I read to Eric, and thus modeled a reading strategy, contained his name. The text was about a boy who had a baby sister, just like he did. Eric liked to see himself in the texts. This provided many opportunities for him to make connections to the literature and feel a part of it.

Instructional Methods That Helped Eric Develop Reading Strategies

Because Eric was puzzled by what readers do when they read, the instructional methods that I used involved modeling what readers can do when they are stuck. The lessons we worked on focused on explicit teaching, showing Eric how to implement reading strategies. Eric learned that rereading books through repeated readings would help him become a better reader and "own" many new words. He looked forward to rereading books, and together we kept track of his improvements over time. It surprised me too, that during one of his LEA stories, he used two words in his story that he was having difficulty with. He seemed to know that using these words in new contexts, as he often saw me do to review words, would make them a part of his permanent reading vocabulary. In addition, the strategies I chose built on his existing strengths. Repeated readings worked because I recognized that although he had a hard time remembering word families, he did remember whole words that were introduced in context. Eric was keenly aware that words are spelled a specific way, so I provided him with a word bank or the strategy to underline a word when he knew that he hadn't spelled the word correctly.

Eric evolved from a boy who pretended to be a reader to one who could read. Although he continued to struggle with some of the phonics instruction in his classroom program, once he learned words fluently by sight, he never forgot them, and this began to help him make connections with words that shared similar patterns. At the end of the school year, he and his classmates wrote me thank-you letters. Although many of his classmates thanked me for reading to them and wrote that they liked the word games we played, Eric's letter was different.

Than you for helping me to be a good reader.

Love,
Eric Anthony H.

References

Au, K. H. (1998). Social constructivism and the school literacy learning of students of diverse backgrounds. *Journal of Literacy Research, 30*, 297–319.

Clay, M. (1986). *The early detection of reading difficulties, with recovery procedures* (3rd ed). Portsmouth, NH: Heinemann.

Cunningham, P. (1999). What should we do about phonics? In L. Gambrell, L. Morrow, S. Neuman, & M. Pressley (Eds.) *Best practices in literacy instruction* (pp. 68–89). New York: Guilford.

Dorr, R. E. (2006). Something old is new again: Revisiting language experience. *The Reading Teacher, 60* (2), 138–146.

Goodman, Y., Watson, D., & Burke, C. (1987). *Reading miscue inventory: Alternative procedures*. New York: Owen.

Johns, J. L. (1997). *Basic reading inventory* (5th ed). Dubuque, IA: Kendall/Hunt.

Novick, R. (2000). Supporting early literacy development: Doing things with words in the real world. *Childhood Education, 76* (2), 70–75.

Peters, C. (1995). *Friends*. Boston: Houghton Mifflin.

Peters, C. (1995). *My dog Willy*. Boston: Houghton Mifflin.

Samuels, S. J. (1997). The method of repeated readings. *Reading Teacher, 50* (5), 376–381.

Seuss, Dr. (1960). *Green eggs and ham*. New York: Random House.

Yopp, H. K. (1995). A test for assessing phonemic awareness in young children. *The Reading Teacher, 49*, 20–29.

3 | Teaching the Basics of Language Learning

Developing a First Grader's Early Literacy Skills

Judy Stephenson, Literacy Specialist

"It wasn't that he couldn't talk. He just chose not to."
Judy Stephenson on First Grader, Donnie

When Donnie's first-grade teacher approached me early in the school year, she described him as very quiet with limited basic skills in reading and writing. In the few short months Donnie had been in the classroom, he was beginning to converse more, but he was already showing signs of frustration and was floundering with his daily assignments. His fine motor skills indicated difficulty in letter formation, and he was unaware of his last name or birthday. He was within the average age range for first-grade students, yet he had just spent the previous 2 years in a kindergarten program in another state.

Donnie was well liked by his peers and had developed many friendships, but his language and literacy ability was suspiciously limited. It wasn't that he couldn't talk; he just chose not to. Instead of being involved in conversations, he proceeded to be a passive listener, and on occasions tuned everything out. Work time proved to be a time of great dependence on his teacher, and Donnie's parents were also beginning to question his developmental abilities. It was at this time that I became involved.

 ## The First Hurdle

My initial concern with Donnie was to develop a comfortable relationship so we could get to know each other in an informal and fun environment. Before any formal testing, we went to my classroom two times a week for 2 weeks. Donnie was not shy and was a very cooperative child. Through conversations and games, I discovered that his conversation displayed limited speech. This observation was confirmed by his parents. As the youngest child in a large family, Donnie liked the dependence that older siblings encouraged. His teacher noted that this was also happening in her classroom: because Donnie was well liked, his peers took care of him. Both his teacher and I thought that perhaps the limited use of language was slowly hindering Donnie's development of those early literacy skills.

During one of our early sessions together in my classroom, I noticed that Donnie had difficulty building the alphabet train puzzle. He needed to rely on the alphabet on the wall as a reference point. He could not recite the alphabet song in its entirety and had labored while trying to match the letters to their names. This led me to believe that assessment and analyses would need to include an examination of his basic literacy strengths, and then I would build an individualized literacy program from there.

 ## Knowing Where to Begin

Given the feedback from Donnie's teacher on her classroom observations of Donnie's reading and writing difficulties, along with my own observations, I decided to start at the very beginning. Knowing that I might be dealing with a correlation between Donnie's lack of language usage and his reading and writing ability, I decided to get a really good overall look at his strengths and weaknesses. As a result, I administered the following assessments:

- Phonemic Awareness Inventory (Fitzpatrick, 1997)
- Observation Survey of Early Literacy Achievement (Clay, 1993)

According to research, a child's level of phonemic awareness is an important determinant on their success or failures with reading (Adams, 1990; National Institute of Child Health and Human Development, 2000; Shaywitz, 2003; Stanovich, 1986). "Students need to have a strong understanding of spoken language before they can understand written language. Children need to be able to hear sounds (phonemes), know the positions, and understand the role they [the sounds] play within a word" (Fitzpatrick, 1997, p. 5). The analyses of the results from this inventory would indicate Donnie's strengths in this area and determine any areas that need further development.

The Observation Survey (OS) can be validly implemented to assess components of early reading and writing development (Clay, 1993; Denton, Ciancio, & Fletcher, 2006; Reading Recovery Council of North America, 2004). In addition to Donnie's reading and writing abilities, this test would provide information on his oral language, sound and symbol knowledge, and his awareness of print and book concepts (Clay, 1993).

Results of the Phonemic Awareness Inventory. According to Fitzpatrick (1997), phonemic awareness can be measured on five different levels: rhythm and rhyme, parts of a word, sequence of sounds, separation of sounds, and manipulation of sounds. Donnie's results on each level were as follows:

Level 1: Rhythm and Rhyme—Donnie was able to determine if words spoken orally were the same words or not. He could not tell if two words presented orally were words that rhymed and could not generate rhyming words for orally given words. Donnie had not yet developed the concept of syllables, even with two examples and given answers ("Don-nie-2"). He had difficulty clapping them out and counting the claps, yet in the following test, he could separate compound words given orally into their parts.

Level 2: Parts of a Word—Donnie was able to separate the syllables of compound words into their separate parts, but could not do two-syllable or three-syllable noncompound words (*rain-bow*, but not *col-or*). He could not blend sounds of a given word to determine the whole word (*f-a-t = fat*).

Level 3: Sequence of Sounds—Donnie could hear sounds at the beginning of words, but not sounds in the final or medial position.

Level 4: Separation of Sounds—This was very difficult for Donnie to do. Rather than mentioning each sound or phoneme that he heard in the word, he just repeated the word.

Level 5: Manipulation of Sounds—During phoneme deletion (say *pop*, now say it again without the /p/) and phoneme substitution (say *pop*, now say it again but replace the first sound with an /m/), the task proved to be a foreign territory for him. In some cases, he repeated the word given or did not try anything, even with several examples.

From the results of this Phonemic Awareness Inventory, it was evident that Donnie was lacking in several areas of phonemic awareness. Needless to say, this would be an area in which these early literacy skills would have to be implemented into his program.

Results of the Observation Survey. The Observation Survey consists of six subtests: letter identification, concepts about print, word tests, writing, hearing sounds in words (dictation), and running records (Clay, 1993). As mentioned, this survey has been documented to be reliable and valid (Clay, 1993; Denton et al., 2006; Reading Recovery Council of North America, 2004). With a background as a trained Reading Recovery teacher, I have used the survey with hundreds of children and am confident that the results provide a broad picture of the child's literacy process.

Letter Identification. Donnie was able to recognize the names of 26 capital letters of the alphabet and 25 of 28 lower case letters (*g* and *a* are represented in two different ways). He was confused with *i/l* and *p/q* (visual similarities). When asked to tell me the sounds that are represented by each capital letter, he was only able to identify 13 sounds (*a, k, p, z, b, h, o, c, m, d, n,* and *i*). I did not ask him to initiate any associated words that begin with those letter sounds. His letter or sound recall was not fluent (automaticity), which was a valid point for me to note.

Concepts About Print. This tests a child's knowledge of how a book works (front page, letters or words, left-to-right directionality, top to bottom, return sweep, punctuation, etc.). Of the 23 questions asked, Donnie was able to correctly respond to 10. The areas of concern were visual scanning, specifics such as letters, punctuation, and the hierarchical concepts such as one-to-one matching, differentiating between a letter and a word, and directionality of letters in words. In summary, print awareness was a difficult concept for him.

Word Tests. This subtest asks the child to correctly identify one of the three lists of the 15 most frequently occurring words based on the Dolch sight Word List (Pinnell, Lyons, Young, & Deford, 1987). Donnie was asked to read list B. The words on this list include *sand, to, will, look, he, up, like, in, where, Mr., going, big, go, let, on*. He was unable to identify any of these words.

Writing. During this subtest, the child is asked to write as many known words as he can with or without prompting. Donnie's best attempt to write anything was to try his name. The five letters covered one-half of an 8½ by 11 inch paper and contained one reversal: a *j*, which is a rarely reversed letter (Donnie is a pseudonym). He did not know what his last name was, which demonstrated a weakness in his fine motor skills as well as evidence of a limited written and oral vocabulary.

Hearing Sounds in Words (Dictation). This task allows the observer to count the "child's representation of the sounds (phonemes) by letters (graphemes)" (Clay, 1993, p. 65). This subtest is supposed to encourage the child to record the sounds on his own. However, by the time I administered this subtest, I knew that Donnie was unable to internalize and record independently any sounds with their corresponding symbols. As a result, the responses given were initiated by my repetition of the sounds. In other words, he could record the symbols to some sounds when I said the word slowly, but he did not have the ability to do the task without external support. From the sample, Donnie was able to hear and represent 15 of the 35 sounds. The capital letters indicate what Donnie wrote, and the correct responses are indicated by the matching letters in italics.

THEBSISCNATYU
STHTUMGA

The	bus	is	coming.	It	will	stop	here	to	let	me	get	on.
The	*b s*	*is*	*c*	*n*	*t*	*st*	*h*	*t*		*m*	*g*	

Running Record. Marie Clay (1993) suggests that a running record obtains information about the child's processing of texts on three different levels: an easy text (95–100% correct), an instructional text (90–94% correct), and a hard text (below 90%). Donnie's easy text included level 2, where he was able to match one to one and continue reading a pattern of text. He was also able to use picture cues to determine unknown words. The next level of text was a 3, which proved to be a frustrational level. In spite of limited abilities demonstrated on the other subtests, Donnie's text level ability was in between a level 2 and level 3.

In addition to the OS results, I also wanted to obtain a sample of how Donnie was able to write his thoughts on paper. I learned through our previous conversations that he liked cats, so I convinced him to tell me something about cats. He decided to write The CAT JUMS. (*The cat jumps.*) Because this short sentence was enough of a struggle for him, I decided not to pursue the addition of more information. Each word was unknown, so I provided a model of how to do the word *The*. From the results of the OS, he knew the sound and letter representation for *c*. He printed the *c* without assistance. For the *a* and *t*, as well as with the sounds and letters in *jump*, I had to give him a sample sound and picture cue from a smaller alphabet chart. "a-a-a apple, t-t-t turtle." I also noticed that he might know the sound, but did not know the symbol representation or how to correctly form the letter. He would scan through the entire alphabet to find the right letter. All letters were in capitals, except *The*, which was copied from an example given by me. Just like with his earlier sample of his written name, he had also reversed the letter *j* in *jumps*. Also, he did not hear the *p* sound in *jump*.

Literacy Challenges: Learner and Teacher

The first challenge was an issue of time: when to implement these strategies that he was missing, and how to do this while not interfering with the first-grade curriculum that he also needed to absorb. Donnie's teacher and I felt that at this time, we did not want him pulled out of the classroom for an intervention program because we wanted him immersed in the language and instruction that took place in the classroom. Because his teacher was already implementing a variety of literacy instruction, she was able to include him in small-group teaching settings. In addition to this, I would tutor him once a week after school to give him intense strategy instruction in both reading and writing and create a home program for his parents. His teacher and I would confer on his progress once a week, and I met with his parents for 10 to 15 minutes at the end of every tutoring session. With this many people on board, it would be easy to monitor his progress and obtain a preponderance of continual assessments, as well as make necessary adjustments to his program.

The second challenge was a caution to not overwhelm Donnie with this continual parade of instruction. In the classroom, the other children were also immersed in small-group learning, so this would seem like the protocol of first grade. His parents would read with him every night, and that's just something that we told him all first graders do. Coming to see me needed to be something that he was excited about doing. I needed to design the instruction so it would be intense, but in short spurts, and provide some movement within that hour. Additionally, a snack and a treasure box can go a long way!

Addressing the Challenge

Using the knowledge of early reading and writing processes, analyzing Donnie's strengths and weaknesses in these two areas, and keeping in mind that he needed additional work with his phonemic and phonological awareness, I decided that I would combine the likes of *Recipe for Reading* (Bloom & Traub, 2005), which provided the phonological piece, *Reading Recovery* (Clay, 1993), which involved both reading and writing instruction, and word work activities from the *Four Blocks Program* (Cunningham & Hall, 2001) to help with his print awareness. His weekly lesson plan was divided into various components:

Sound Cards Blending Vowel Intensive	Sight Word Cards
Familiar Reading	Running Record (on back)
Word Work/Decoding	
Writing/Sentence Work	
Other	
Assessments	

Phonological Activities. The beginning of every tutoring session involved ten minutes of sound card instruction. A letter of the alphabet was placed on an index card. These letters were flashed to Donnie, who would rapidly tell me the sound for that letter. Each letter card was placed in one of three piles: beginning sounds (*s, h, v, k, c, y, q, r, w, l, f, j*), vowels in the middle, and ending sounds. Vowel and consonant combinations were added as appropriate. Once the pile of letter cards was finished, these letters in the three piles were flipped over and Donnie would have to tap out each sound, then blend the sound parts (phonemes) to make a nonsense word. As much as I have read about the irrelevance of nonsense words regarding the meaning aspect of reading, the process does help with sound/letter association and rapid recall.

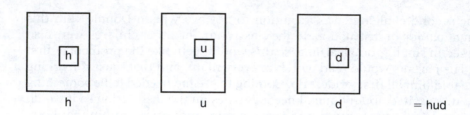

h   u   d   = hud

Once this part was complete, I would say sounds of nonsense words and Donnie would hold up a vowel card that contained the sound of the vowel in the word. These vowel-intensive cards later became his pictorial cuing system for the vowel sounds and letter association (*apple, elephant, igloo, octopus,* and *umbrella*). For example, if I said "zop," he would hold up the *o* card, which had a picture of an octopus on it. This activity encourages a child to hear sounds in words and eventually associate the sounds with a picture or symbol. Using a nonsense word in this activity eliminates the dependence on visually recalling real words and knowing what vowel is represented in that word.

Word Work Activities. Word work and decoding activities for Donnie involved magnetic letters, a magnetic board, dry-erase markers, and a dry-erase whiteboard. We would build words and take them apart with the magnetic letters on the whiteboard at the front of the classroom. This allowed him to get up and move, and the activity was followed by a dictation lesson where he was supposed to rapidly recall how to write his known words. This task proved to be difficult for Donnie as he attempted to maneuver the dry-erase marker on the board. Eventually, it became an easier task for him. These word-making activities were presented in alignment with the sound activities done at the beginning of the lesson, as well as what Donnie was demonstrating when he read or wrote. For example, if I noticed that Donnie was having trouble with the letter *o*, then his activities included words with *o* or shaving cream to make the letter *o* with sound references. The letter *o* would also be enforced within the text of the book. Please note: I did not use books that strictly were to practice that letter; all books were leveled texts in a variety of genres. As short *o* words appeared in the text, Donnie and I would make a list. I wanted to make sure that he was transferring this new knowledge into the context of reading a leveled text rather than a decodable text strictly using the new letter discussed.

Reading Activities. I did not use sight word cards until the third lesson. Donnie's teacher was using them in the classroom, but at this point, I did not know what was in his realm of known words until I could assess these in reading and writing. Because he only knew how to read and write his name on the initial assessment, he evidently had a limited repertoire of known words! Once sight words became part of the lesson, I introduced three new ones each week and "blended" them into his already known word pile. Sometimes they were chosen from the text we read; sometimes they were from his writings. These sight word cards were also read every night at home, and practiced on the whiteboard for writing fluency and recall.

Familiar reading or repeated reading was a very important activity that I wanted to incorporate into the lessons. It encourages fluency and reading rate (Samuels, 1979) as well as to help students feel comfortable when acquiring a new language (Baker et al., 1999). I felt that Donnie's reading process was similar to his acquisition of a new language: book language. Donnie would pick three books from his pile of books that were read at home and reread them to me. These leveled books contained predictable language with some gradient of difficulty throughout increasing levels (Clay, 1993). During this time, it was very important for Donnie to also be immersed in discussion regarding the meaning of the story.

Immediately following the familiar readings, I would do a running record on the new text that was introduced and read the previous week. The reason for using a "seen text, is that we want to see how well the reader orchestrates the various kinds of reading behaviors he controls, given that this reading is being guided by the meaningfulness of the text" (Clay, 1993, p. 23).

All of the running records done with Donnie were not always done with "seen" texts. Occasionally, I would do a cold reading on a Reading Recovery leveled book to check his processing at the current level or pick a correlating level from the *Developmental Reading Assessment* (DRA) (Beaver, 1997). The DRA provided information on his text-level processing ability with more than one book and also informed me whether I should move him up to the next level or not.

Discussion is an essential factor for immersing the child in language as he works through the text, demonstrating the strategies he has previously learned. Ultimately, this is an important teaching time to reinforce what you see the child doing as he processes the text. For example, I may say, "You knew there was a word that tricked you, and I love how you went back, checked the picture again, checked the letters again, and figured it out. That's what good readers do." In my mind, I would also do an informal running record to double-check that the text I was using was an appropriate level for him. There is a fine line between support needed and a text that is too difficult.

Writing and Sentence Activities. As the lesson plan components indicate, the content of the lessons involved interspersing the activities within each other. In other words, I did not do all phonological activities first, then reading activities, then the writing component. Instead, all of the activities were intermingled to enhance the process and to demonstrate to Donnie that all of these components work together. This also provided the much-needed breaks in his instructional time.

Donnie was very efficient in creating an idea for stories. The difficulty surfaced when he had to write the words. Since his vocabulary was limited and his letter sound knowledge needed guidance, this was a difficult task for him. His fine motor skills, as mentioned, were weak when it came to letter formation and size. He relied on the alphabet chart to locate the letter and notice how it was formed. Needless to say, it was evident that this was not his favorite part of the lesson.

Fitting Instruction to Meet the Needs of the Child

I am a firm believer that a particular program or "one size fits all" instruction is not necessarily structured to fit the needs of every child. Combining components from various programs, strategies, or philosophies gave me a much more tailored approach for Donnie. I would not be aware of these needed components if I did not use continual assessments and careful analyses of his processes. Therefore, I had to be aware of his ongoing literacy development and make sure my lessons encouraged further growth.

Phonological Awareness and Word Work. As Donnie made progress with his letter/sound connections, new letters and sounds were introduced. In the beginning, as mentioned, Donnie knew 13 of the 26 sounds provided by single letters of the alphabet (I did not attempt consonant or vowel digraphs at that point). Because we were only meeting once every week, I had to rely on Donnie's teacher and his parents to also be encouraging the letter sound connections. So, every week when he would come to me, there were a few newly acquired sounds and symbols, and some that I knew he would need before others. This is when I would use shaving cream for letter formation and sound stimulation, "O (make a circle) says *oh*." On occasion, I would also use sandpaper letters for him to trace with his finger.

Careful monitoring of his letter formation indicated when I had to also provide a change in my instruction. I noticed that he had difficulty differentiating between a *p* and a *b*. What I was trying to show him was not working. Because most of his printing was with capital letters, it was a known "hook" for him to remember that the *b* just has the top bump missing (*B*). Later I could use it as a reference in a familiar word. "You know how to write the word *be* that starts with the letter *b*."

Gradually, I could introduce more letter sounds and symbols. During the fourth lesson, he wanted to write the word *brother* in his story and he knew it began with a *br*. So for the next lesson, I decided to introduce blends, using the consonants that he already knew (*br*, *st*, *sp*). These were added to the sound card part of the lesson as well. Eventually, I was able to add more blends as well as some digraphs. Once I did this, I also incorporated some word work lessons to match. Using the *Making Words* activities book (Cunningham & Hall, 2001), I was able to pull out those lessons to reinforce the concepts that we were learning.

Additionally, by the ninth lesson, Donnie was able to hear and reproduce the short vowel sounds of *a*, *o*, and *u*, but had trouble discriminating between the short vowel sound of *e* and *i*. By this time, he knew the sounds of the consonants and could distinguish between them in the initial and final positions. Therefore, we changed our word work to focus on sounds in the middle of the word, both consonants and vowels. There was not a lesson available to provide for this, so using the structure of the *Making Words* activity (Cunningham & Hall, 2001), I was able to create a lesson.

> sat—sit, pat—pit, pan—pin, etc.

Reading. Donnie's growth in reading involved both sight words in isolation and in text as well as his decoding of unknown words. By the 15th lesson, Donnie's sight word pile had grown to 60 known words in reading. His decoding ability did not progress as quickly. Because he had difficulty connecting letters and symbols fluently both in reading and writing, this was going to be an area of intense instruction.

I noticed that as we advanced through the levels of text, he also needed more strategies. By the time Donnie was reading texts on levels 7 and 8, he could no longer just rely on the picture clues and his known sight words. He actually had to be using some visual analysis techniques while cross checking those meaning and visual clues (Clay, 1993). For example, during the 16th lesson, Donnie was reading on level 8. The character in the story was at a grocery store. He came upon the word *cart*. He read the word as *buggy*. Although it made sense, it was time for him to be using his visual letter cues as well. Without me even saying a word, he said, "No, that's not *buggy*, it's *cart*." This was the first time I noticed that he was using the new strategy. As soon as the story was over, I reinforced this concept to him. The next time we read, I reminded him about what he had done and that he might need to do it again in other books. I had to be careful to enforce the meaning of reading along with the visual cuing and decoding strategies to avoid Donnie seeing the process of reading as just calling and sounding out words.

Again, as Donnie was required to process more difficult words, the word work section of the lesson was adjusted as well. About this time, I started to do more work with word endings and visually similar words. This was to enforce him to track the letters sequentially across a whole word and to use a new strategy that encouraged him to recognize parts (chunks) of the word (known parts) to help him discover the unknown word.

Writing.   Although Donnie's reading ability was improving, his writing ability progressed at a slower pace. Donnie could read many of his sight words in isolation as well as when the words were embedded in text, but his fluent writing of sight words needed additional instruction. We would use three new sight words a week and practice writing them on the board with the markers. Although this was successful, he occasionally did not transfer this knowledge into his written seat work. As a result, he would also have to practice it on a small board at his seat and write it three times in his writing book. This also became a task for his parents to work on at home.

At first, with his writing book, I began by accepting very short, sometimes three-word, sentences. Later, I would encourage more and more. As time unfolded, he was beginning to internalize more sounds and was able to write words more quickly. I began to give him spaces to show how many sounds he should have. For example, if he was writing *can*, I would say "It has to fit here _____ _____ _____."

On occasion, when I was introducing new sounds and letters, he needed a visual cue or another modality. For example, we were working on *th*. Because he knew the word *the*, I thought this would be a good hook. However, he was not responsive to that. So we learned it as the letter combination that makes his tongue touch the space where he was missing his front teeth. When he would print a word that had the *th* sound, I could see him maneuvering his tongue to that spot.

Initially, I gave him a home-made writing book that was made of 8½ by 11 inch paper. As his fine motor skills developed, I would draw lines for him. By the ninth lesson, he had "graduated to using the big-boy, first-grade paper" which already had the D'Nealian lines printed on it. At this time, his sentences writing ventured from simple patterns (*The cat*) to attempting more difficult words within a pattern. On that day, he wrote *I like red pretend puppies*. (He had checked out a Clifford book from the library.)

By the 14th lesson, he was writing words and sounds on his own as well as expanding his stories (with some encouragement of course). He did not use the alphabet chart anymore and was beginning to use more lowercase letters without me reminding him.

I ueNt to MichiGN. (I went to Michigan.)

I PLAD in the SNO. (I played in the snow.)

I MADE A SNOMAN. (I made a snowman.)

On the 17th lesson, we hit a milestone! He usually came in, sat down, and ate his cookies while I was getting all of his things ready. He told me that he did not want to eat his cookies yet because he wanted to finish writing his book. He had taken some paper, folded it in half, and put about 20 staples down the fold, and inside he had written a patterned story similar to *Brown Bear, Brown Bear* by Bill Martin Jr. He proceeded to write the next four pages before he was satisfied. Then he read it to me. This was the first indication that he had even wanted to write!

By the 20th lesson, Donnie was well on his way to independent writing at the first-grade level. I had introduced the concept of pounding and tapping (Bloom & Traub, 2005). This is where he is to clap or pound out the syllables, and tap out the sounds in each syllable. Without any assistance from me, he wrote his story.

> MY fAfVroIt gam is POKeaMON. (My favorite game in Pokemon.)
> MY faFVroIt part is RoNING ShIOS. (My favorite part is running shoes.)

At this point, I could see a huge growth in his independent writing ability compared to The CAT JUMS at the beginning, when I had to say the sounds of the word slowly and he had to use the alphabet chart to find the letter. More important, he began to see the communicative properties of writing, as in his retelling of his trip to Michigan and his self-authored pattern book, rather than seeing writing as a tedious and difficult task.

In summary, Donnie's literacy behaviors guided the degree of intensity and content within his lessons. Keeping in mind that effective literacy practices in research involve all areas and not just one concept in isolation, I had to incorporate these into the lessons. (I told him that reading and writing were best friends!) The individual lessons helped Donnie to see the overall picture of literacy in his first-grade classroom as well as one-on-one with me. He was speaking more, reading independently, and not hesitating to write. Additionally, he was also driven by the fact that every baby step along the way was magnified when he recognized his own success with each new concept.

References

Adams, M. J. (1990). *Beginning to read: Thinking and learning about print*. Cambridge, MA: MIT Press.

Baker, T. K., Bisson, I. H., Blum, T. S., Creamer, T. S., Koskinen, P. S., & Phillips, S. M. (1999). Shared reading books and audiotapes: Supporting diverse students in school and at home. *The Reading Teacher, 52*, 430–444.

Beaver, J. (1997). *Developmental reading assessment*. Parsippany, NJ: Celebration Press.

Bloom, F., & Traub, N. (2005). *Recipe for reading: Intervention strategies for struggling readers*. Cambridge, MA: Educators Publishing Service.

Clay, M. (1993). *An observation survey of early literacy achievement.* Portsmouth, NH: Heinemann.

Cunningham, P. M., & Hall, D. P. (2001). *Making words: Lessons for home or school grade 1.* Greensboro, NC: Carson-Dellosa.

Denton, C. A., Ciancio, D. J., & Fletcher, J. M. (2006). Validity, reliability, and utility of the Observation Survey of Early Literacy Achievement. *Reading Research Quarterly, 41,* 8–34.

Fitzpatrick, J. (1997). *Phonemic awareness: Playing with sounds to strengthen beginning reading skills.* Cypress, CA: Creative Teaching Press.

National Institute of Child Health and Human Development. (2000). *Report of the National Reading Panel: Teaching children to read: An evidence-based assessment of the scientific research literature on reading and its implications for reading instruction* (NIH Publication No. 00-4769). Washington, DC: U.S. Government Printing Office.

Pinnell, G. S., Lyons, C. A., Young, P., & Deford, D. E. (1987). *The Reading Recovery Program in Ohio.* Columbus, OH: Columbus State University.

Reading Recovery Council of North America (2004*). Standards and guidance of the Reading Recovery Council of North America.* (4th ed.). Columbus, OH: Author.

Samuels, S. J. (1979). The method of repeated reading. *The Reading Teacher, 32,* 403–408.

Shaywitz, S. (2003). *Overcoming dyslexia.* New York: Vintage Books.

Stanovich, K. E. (1986). Matthew effects in reading: Some consequences of individual differences in the acquisition of literacy. *Reading Research Quarterly, 21,* 360–406.

4 | Expanding Vocabulary

Motivating a Third-Grade Student to Learn and Use New Words

Jaime Berry, Third-Grade Teacher

"I forgot what I was going to say."
Third Grader, Tina

Tina often struggled to make herself clear in her talk and in her writing because of what I believed was a limited vocabulary. She was a friendly, talkative, and determined third-grade student. She appeared to enjoy her work, and she was eager for both reading and writing time. Yet Tina had significant trouble in all subject areas and had been identified as at-risk by the previous year's assessments. When I met with Tina for our first writing conference, I noted that she had wonderful ideas but struggled to find words in which to express them, often resulting in stories that were more like lists. During class I frequently observed how my students talked about their individual reading, the books I read to them and the stories they wrote. I noticed that Tina seldom participated in these conversations. When she attempted to contribute she struggled to express her thoughts verbally and often gave up, frequently saying, "I forgot what I was going to say."

The First Hurdle: Tina's Loss for Words

In Tina's first writing conference, she read me the story she was working on. She had written a list of events that occurred over her summer vacation, not uncommon for emerging writers. I asked her why this story was important to her. Tina told me she and her cousin had been swimming, swallowed water, and been rescued by an uncle. I asked her if she thought she could write about that part. She tried, but instead ended up with a more elaborate list with only a few sentences dedicated to the incident she wanted to write about. When we conferenced again she indicated again that the swimming incident was the most important part, but that she didn't know how to describe it. I could see that Tina wanted to tell her story, but as in all of my previous observations, her limited vocabulary interfered with her desire to express herself. I realized that part of her struggle was her inexperience as a writer, but if I could do something to improve her vocabulary she might enjoy more success in reading, writing, and her conversations with others.

 # Knowing Where to Begin

Tina had significant trouble in all subject areas and had been identified as an at-risk student based on initial assessments in vocabulary, reading fluency, reading comprehension, sight words, listening comprehension, and writing. I believed that her limited vocabulary played a role in holding her back as a reader and writer and felt that the curriculum did little to build my students' vocabulary. I did teach "vocabulary strategies" as part of our curriculum for the literacy block to give my students strategies for figuring out unfamiliar words when they encountered them in a text. These lessons were meant to increase a child's reading comprehension by enhancing vocabulary development subskills through active reading. Subskills that increase vocabulary development include the following tasks: classifying words, providing synonyms, providing antonyms, recognizing some words' multiple meanings, comparing words, and describing or defining words (Johnston, Tulbert, Sebastian, Devries, & Gombert, 2000). However, I noticed that teaching these subskills did little to increase my students' motivation and excitement about word learning, and it seemed that though my struggling readers like Tina could recite the taught strategies, they seldom used them.

What Does the Research Say?

Although I became more aware of the fact that vocabulary plays such an important role in either limiting or accelerating my students as readers and writers, I knew little of what I could do to enhance my current literacy curriculum. I turned to the research to explore how to teach vocabulary in meaningful ways. First I wanted to understand how words are learned and what it means to know a word. I learned that what counts as a student's vocabulary can be defined in many ways, from recognizing a word to being able to use the word in speech and writing and to discuss a word in relation to other words and concepts (Beck, McKeown, & Kucan, 2002; Beck, McKeown, & Omanson, 1987; Nagy & Scott, 2000).

One point that reoccurred in the research is that learning is increased when the instructional techniques rely on active rather than passive student involvement. Providing language learning opportunities through meaningful activities in the classroom is more effective than using more passive instructional counterparts, especially for students with little prior knowledge when encountering an unfamiliar word (Ewers & Brownson, 1999; Hadley, Simmerman, Long, & Luna, 2000). Although my instruction included many lessons on active reading or strategies for word learning in context, I was convinced that the kids in my class were unengaged and that these strategies did little good for Tina and my other struggling readers.

Students who struggle in my class in reading and writing naturally have limited vocabularies, and they in turn are limited in their ability to participate in and contribute to class discussions or group work that occurs throughout the day. It is in the upper elementary grades that students become aware of their limitations, become frustrated and eventually become unmotivated toward any literacy experiences (Roberts, 1999). Research shows that vocabulary knowledge is strongly related to reading comprehension, academic achievement, and overall intellectual ability (Ewers & Brownson, 1999; McKeown, Beck, Omanson, & Perfetti, 1983). Therefore, it seemed important that I do something now for Tina and my other struggling readers that would engage them in word learning.

Get Kids to Talk About Words

A child *needs both* to have an idea of what a word means, integrating information for meaning construction by accessing background experiences, and make connections between words (Rupley, Logan, & Nichols, 1999). While active reading strategies undoubtedly promote this integration, it seems that conversation would naturally lend itself to this integration as well. Winters (2000) argues that there are three essential understandings in current research related to early vocabulary and concept development. The first, concept development, is a problem-solving process where children relate a new idea by comparing and contrasting it to their existing knowledge; the second, concept learning, is an integration of not only semantic information but also place, context, and emotion; and last; social interaction must take place to increase concept development. It is thought that an opportunity to verbalize forming concepts is essential for children in cementing their new knowledge (Winters, 2000).

Similarly, Brabham and Villaume (2002) assert that not only do reading aloud to children and a child's own independent reading contribute to vocabulary growth through incidental learning, but conversation plays a large role in vocabulary development as well. When students discuss, it provides an opportunity for those children who might not automatically do so to activate prior knowledge and gain access to a difficult or an intimidating word through discussion. Reading to learn a word's meaning in context for kids who struggle is less successful than talk or brainstorming with a small group regarding activating prior knowledge (Harmon & Hedrick, 2000). Similarly, I identified with the students discussed by Ruddell and Shearer (2002), who found that struggling students typically had little interest in words they encountered in context and were therefore unmotivated to use any active reading strategies in order to figure them out. They found that using the Vocabulary Self-Collection Strategy (VSS), allowing the children to choose the words they studied and discuss them with the class, significantly increased student motivation, interest, and word meaning retention.

As I read the research, I realized that although my teaching did include instruction in building active reading strategies, I was not providing any time during the week for my students to discuss and share the new vocabulary they had acquired. I was relying on activities such as wide reading and the use of independent word learning strategies to learn word meanings and to understand concepts. Although this incidental exposure is a way in which many children learn new words, I had not considered that students like Tina who struggled with reading were typically unable to do either activity with successful results (Bryant, Goodwin, Bryant, & Higgins, 2003).

 ## Literacy Challenges: Learner and Teacher

Tina's constant struggle to write and express herself during book talks led me to question my teaching and consider how I was neglecting to find the time to provide high-interest activities that required word learning and concept building. After exploring the literature on current vocabulary instruction, I was even more certain that I was not addressing the needs of my struggling students regarding their vocabulary development. Considering these flaws in my current teaching practices, I decided to incorporate specific time to "word research" as part of our literacy block. In particular, I based it on the Vocabulary Self-Collection Strategy (Ruddell & Shearer, 2002). As I employed this new type of vocabulary instruction, I took careful notes on Tina, to see how effective this approach was for improving vocabulary.

 ## Addressing the Challenge
Adding Word Research to Our Literacy Block

I began by introducing a time of the day specifically dedicated to what I called "word research" to distinguish it from our normal word study dedicated primarily to increasing decoding and spelling knowledge. Normally, I taught word research as part of the literacy block. I was able to add word research twice a week for about 30 minutes a session. In the beginning I modeled finding an unfamiliar word in the classroom; the word was *evacuation* from the sign above the fire drill map in our room. I then modeled how I might try to figure out its meaning by thinking aloud, using several of the subskills of vocabulary development (Johnston et al., 2000). Students were then to find a word some time that day from any place they liked; this built their interest and excitement. Later, I divided them into four groups, where they were to tell

- where they found their word
- why they chose it

- what they thought the word meant
- how they came to an understanding of the word's meaning.

They were instructed to talk with their group to come up with a definition. I documented this initially by having them write their reasons for choosing a word, its meaning, and where they found it on an index card. They struggled with adequately putting their ideas down in writing; so I often asked them and recorded their responses to document progress, with particular attention to the word research group that included Tina. After the first session, students were allowed to bring in a word from anywhere they liked and were encouraged to discuss its possible meaning with someone in their family rather than looking it up in the dictionary; these words were then mixed up and split among the groups to be discussed and defined, building their personal investment in the experience.

The words they brought in were posted on a chart by their names. They were then given time to discus their word in a small group. My students were used to talking in small groups and had worked in groups on various projects in different content areas. However, they had never discussed word meanings or their strategies for figuring them out. Initially their conversations were not rich, but as I modeled in whole group lesson what they were expected to do, their conversations gradually improved. I taught several lessons on what it meant to work in a group and be a good partner. As the groups talked, one member was responsible for writing the definition they developed as a group. We then met as a class to share definitions and get feedback from other classmates to improve definitions. During our nonfiction unit, they were to find words in the books they were reading in order to strongly connect the vocabulary to the content studied and to allow them to have the word in context.

Measuring Tina's Progress in Word Learning and Participation

I audiotaped Tina's group discussions during word research time or took notes on her participation in small-group and whole-group discussions during other parts of the day. I wanted to look at how adding a time for my students to study word meanings would increase Tina's vocabulary development and her participation in discussions. I looked at how often Tina made contributions to the group's word discussions and what strategies she used to help figure out word meanings (prior knowledge, synonyms, recognizing multiple meanings, etc.).

When the groups began, Tina's talk was minimal and she rarely helped her group define an unfamiliar word. But as time went on, Tina grew in her participation. In this excerpt, Tina was initiating ideas for the first time and not relying on other group members to prompt her thinking. In this meeting the students were discussing the word *introduction*.

TINA: This one is like when you tell your name to the class and it's in books.

CASSANDRA: Yeah, in the beginning of a book sometimes.

JOSEPH: So it means . . . what?

TINA: Like to say hello or in the beginning of the book.

CASSANDRA: Not to say hello.

TINA: (Interrupts) Yes! It means like say your name too.

In many conversations Tina used prior knowledge, provided synonyms, and gave descriptions or the contexts of how words would be used. Later she progressed to helping the group think about multiple ways that a word could be used, as in the conversation about the word *cold-blooded*, which occurred during our nonfiction unit of study.

TINA: *Cold-blooded* is when you're mean.

JOSEPH: But here it means about animals.

CASSANDRA: Like snakes and lizards they have to be warm by being in the sun. If they're not in the sun they get too cold because their blood is cold. That is what it means.

TINA: Well, I think it can mean that you're not nice too.

JOSEPH: Yeah, I think she's right.

Tina continued to increase in her participation during word research time. She continued to make contributions to a better understanding of the word by providing contexts for the word and clarifying other group members' ideas. When discussing the word *hallelujah*, Tina shares where the word is used and also challenges what the word means by sharing an example of a member of her family who uses the word.

JOSEPH: You say it when you're happy.

TINA: Like people say it in church. They sing it to God.

JOSEPH: It means you love God.

TINA: I don't know what it means. My auntie says it a lot when she worries.

As students became used to the routine of discussing new words they became more skilled in clarifying what a word meant. Here Tina and her group progress from their initial idea that a reflection is a shadow to seeing your image in something that reflects.

JOSEPH: It's like your shadow.

TINA: But it's your shadow but your picture in a mirror.

CASSANDRA: Not your shadow but your picture in a mirror

TINA: Like seeing yourself in the mirror

CASSANDRA: . . . or in water or something.

When groups brought in words, their discussions of context for the words were usually given from their prior knowledge, as when discussing the word *hallelujah* when Auntie worries or remembering that *cold-blooded* can also be used as a synonym for *mean*. Rarely did they act on these conjectures to create clearer contexts. During the nonfiction unit study when students were asked to select words from the books that they were reading during independent reading time, the students made greater use of context and often learned more about a word, based on that context. In this conversation, Tina's group discussed the word *fossil*. Tina draws the group's attention to a book that describes how fossils can be reassembled to show us what prehistoric creatures looked like.

CASSANDRA: Fossils are dinosaur's bones.

TINA: But they're old.

JOSEPH: And they're in the dirt or in caves.

ERNESE: Yeah, they have to dig them up.

TINA: Then they put them together. See? (Shows group picture in book).

Overall, Tina did progress in becoming more expressive in class, as exhibited by her participation in her word research, small-group, and whole-group discussions. For the first 3 months of implementing word research, I documented Tina's participation during her word research group and during whole-class discussions. Only meaningful and appropriate contributions were counted. During the month of November she participated 7 times in her small group and 3 times during our whole-class discussions. In December she made a contribution 17 times during her small-group discussions and 11 times in our whole-group discussions. In January Tina continued her strong participation by making 22 contributions to small-group discussions and 12 contributions to our whole-class discussions. Although I did not track her increased participation in other settings, I believe that her increased confidence and willingness to participate in other discussions and express herself verbally would show similar results.

The most recurring observations I noticed since starting word research was all of my students' increased level of engagement and excitement. It was difficult for me to keep the sessions to the planned 30-minute time frame because the students wanted to keep discussing their words and wanted more words to discuss. I found the small-group discussion contained much more focused talk than did small-group discussions about other topics in the day. It was rare for a group to stray off task. Several of my students, including Tina, requested that we do word research more often and brought in additional words they'd collected.

Limited Impact on Tina's Reading and Writing

I also wanted to see if there was evidence that the word learning influenced her growth as a reader and writer. To do this, I looked for progress during her reading and writing conferences, reviewed her writing pieces, and kept track of her reading level by doing running records. Overall, I did not see measurable progress in these areas that I could attribute to the attention to vocabulary/word research.

In the beginning of the year my conference documentation showed that Tina relied most heavily on decoding by initial letter sounds than by using meaning or context when encountering unfamiliar words. Later in the year, she did improve by using synonyms for unknown words or rereading sentences as an additional strategy for figuring out words. This could be attributed to the word-solving lessons and coaching I gave throughout the year and perhaps to her increased attention to thinking about word meanings. However, her overall reading level did not improve significantly.

With respect to Tina's writing growth, I did not see any evidence of the word research experience influencing her writing. She did not include any of the words studied by her group in her writing pieces, nor did she use any of the words that she studied in the nonfiction unit to include in her own nonfiction report. Many of my other students did use their word research words in their reports. In fact, of the class of 22 children, 17 related used the words and topics they discussed and utilized the studied vocabulary words in their nonfiction writing projects.

Lessons Learned

Overall, I think adding the word research component to our literacy block made a great impact on my students. I saw the greatest improvement in Tina's interest in learning and her willingness to participate and express her ideas verbally in both small-group and whole-class discussions. This was a huge obstacle for Tina at the beginning of the year, where she would consistently get flustered and give up by saying "I forgot." Tina went from infrequent participation to asserting her ideas and even redirecting her peers' thinking. My next challenge is to find ways to extend Tina's progress and enthusiasm into her reading and writing. I do realize that the verbal expression needed to come first, and that transfer to reading and writing often takes longer.

 ## Fitting Instruction to Meet the Needs of the Child

Making time to talk about new vocabulary was extremely valuable and enjoyable to the children in my class. The level of excitement surrounding "word research" in my classroom was high. My kids continue to bring in words to class to add to our chart and share with their peers. Just as Ruddell and Shearer

(2002) found in their study, giving the children a sense of investment and ownership in their learning positively effects their motivation. Through their talk they were able to accurately define unfamiliar words. Tina accumulated strategies she observed her classmates using, she participated, and she questioned and thought critically. She contributed in valuable ways in her small-group discussions and in whole-class discussions; many times she provided information that resulted in helping her group understand and develop a connection to a new word. Talk with a small group functioned as a gateway for Tina. The discussions in small groups provided a nonintimidating opportunity for the children to integrate their personal experiences and make connections between and to words (Rupley et al., 1999).

I found that for third graders, removing the word from context and having them self-report context often impeded their ability to develop meaning. On the other hand, I also noted in my journal that when I allowed students to have free rein to choose a word, they showed the greatest excitement and "owned" the experience. Some pulled words from songs, church, and signs in the neighborhood. They relied more heavily on their prior knowledge and synonym replacement than on closely examining the context. This is something that I need to work on next. I recently read about an instructional approach called "Find that Word" in which students are given a word and challenged to find a word being used in texts, speech, and so forth (Richek, 2005). This might help them to see the value of context, when choosing their own words.

I also found through my observations of Tina and the rest of the students that their social interactions gave a context for students to spend more time talking about a word or concept (Winters, 2000). Not only did Tina and students show greater participation in talking about words, but I also observed that they spent more time stopping to think about their ideas while constructing meaning. As a teacher, one thing I will continue to do is provide a time of the day where the class discusses new vocabulary in a small-group setting. These discussions were incredibly focused, generated accurate definitions, and gave all kids a chance to contribute. All students were excited about learning new words from each other and on some level were able to access new words through the skills they developed in their word investigations.

References

Beck, I. L., McKeown, M. G., & Kucan, L. (2002). Bringing words to life: Robust vocabulary instruction. New York: Guilford.

Beck, I. L., McKeown, M. G., & Omanson, R. C. (1987). The effects and uses of diverse vocabulary instructional techniques. In M. G. McKeown & M. E. Curtis (Eds.), *The nature of vocabulary acquisition* (pp. 147–163). Hillsdale, NJ: Erlbaum.

Brabham, E. G., & Villaume, S. K. (2002). Vocabulary instruction: Concerns and visions. *The Reading Teacher, 56*(3), 264–268.

Bryant, D. P., Goodwin, M., Bryant, B. R., & Higgins, K. (2003). Vocabulary instruction for students with learning disabilities: A review of the research. *Learning Disability Quarterly, 26,* 117–128.

Ewers, C. A., & Brownson, S. M. (1999). Kindergarteners' vocabulary acquisition as a function of active vs. passive storybook reading, prior vocabulary, and working memory. *Journal of Reading Psychology, 20,* 11–20.

Hadley, P. A., Simmerman, A., Long, M., & Luna, M. (2000). Facilitating language development for inner-city children: Experimental evaluation of a collaborative, classroom-based intervention. *Language, Speech, and Hearing Services in Schools, 31,* 280–295.

Harmon, J. M., & Hedrick, W. B. (2000). Zooming in and zooming out: Enhancing vocabulary and conceptual learning in social studies. *The Reading Teacher, 54*(2), 155–159.

Johnston, S. S., Tulbert, B. L., Sebastian, J. P., Devries, K., & Compert, A. (2000). Vocabulary development: A collaborative effort for teaching content vocabulary. *Intervention in School and Clinic, 35,* 311–315.

McKeown, M. G., Beck, I. L., Omanson, R. C., & Perfetti, C. A. (1983). The effects of long-term vocabulary instruction on reading comprehension: A replication. *Journal of Reading Behavior, 15*(1), 3–18.12.

Nagy, W. E., & Scott, J. A. (2000). Vocabulary processes. In M. L. Kamil, P. B. Mosenthal, D. Pearson, & R. Barr (Eds.), *Handbook of reading research* (Vol. III, pp. 69–284). Mahwah, NJ: Erlbaum.

Richek, M. (2005). Words are wonderful: Interactive, time-efficient strategies to teach meaning vocabulary. *The Reading Teacher, 58,* 414–423.

Roberts, E. (1999). Critical teacher thinking and imaginations: Uncovering two vocabulary strategies to increase comprehension. *Reading Horizons, 40*(1), 65–77.

Ruddell, M. R., & Shearer, B. A. (2002). "Extraordinary", "tremendous", "exhilarating", "magnificent": Middle school at-risk students become avid word learners with Vocabulary Self-Collection Strategy (VSS). *Journal of Adolescent & Adult Literacy, 45,* 352–363.

Rupley, W. H., Logan, J. W., & Nichols, W. D. (1999). Vocabulary instruction in a balanced reading program. *The Reading Teacher, 52,* 336–346.

Winters, R. (2000). Vocabulary anchors: Building conceptual connection with young readers. *The Reading Teacher, 54,* 659–662.

5 | Creating Purposeful Literacy Contexts

Engaging a Fourth Grader in Strategic Reading
Through Cross-Age Tutoring

Melissa Agnetti, Fourth-Grade Teacher

"After I teach the strategy, I feel like I know it better!"
Fourth Grader, Maria

At the beginning of every school year, I take the time to observe my fourth-grade students during independent reading time so that I can witness their reading habits and familiarity with books. Maria was a student who raised my concern very early. As I observed her with her self-selected text, I noticed that she would look around the classroom rather than at her book. During these first weeks, I also spent time interviewing my students to get an idea of their perception of themselves as readers. I asked the students to bring a book with them to the conferences so I could note their book choices and see how it compared to their actual reading abilities. Maria brought *Harry Potter and the Goblet of Fire* (Rowling, 2000) to our first conference. I noted that her book choice was above a fourth-grade reading level with hundreds of pages. As I began our conference, I asked Maria what made her pick this particular book. Maria responded, "I like to read books with many pages." I asked Maria why and she said, "Because they are hard, and only good readers could read them." I continued to discuss with Maria the book and her reading preferences. I asked, "Do you like reading?" and she looked down and stated, "Not really!" I was not surprised by her answer. It was no wonder that she didn't like to read, because her selections were based on what looked impressive to others and not by what she could actually read. Maria seemed to be spending too much time on looking like a good reader than actually choosing to read for enjoyment.

 ## The First Hurdle: Reading Is Not All About the Number of Pages

As I continued to conference with Maria each week, I asked her to read a few pages of her book to me and to summarize what she read. Maria was choppy when reading aloud and she seemed to talk about things that never

51

happened in the story. I also noticed that she appeared upset when trying to summarize the pages read. It seemed to me that she knew that she did not understand the story and was embarrassed. From her reading interview and actions it was clear that Maria defined good readers by the number of book pages they read. In her mind, if you were seen reading a book with many pages, others would think that you were a good reader. She stated, "I'm reading this book because it is hard. My brother in sixth grade is reading it at home."

I introduced Maria to books on her reading level, but she continued to choose high-level books that she did not comprehend. During a conference with Maria I asked, "Do you feel that you understand what is happening in this book?" She looked down at her desk and answered, "Not really!" Again Maria seemed embarrassed that she could not understand what she was reading, and it seemed that she was trying to hide it from others. I noticed that when students engaged in conversation about their books, Maria would often volunteer how many pages were in her book.

One day, after a mini-lesson on how readers make connections, I conferenced with Maria during independent reading time to notice her strategy use. She stopped reading and stated, "I would like to make a connection . . . ummmm . . . ," but was unable to actually do so. I realized that Maria could parrot the procedure, but didn't know how to use the strategy to think about texts. She attempted the strategy because she knew that was what I expected her to do, not because she saw this as an effective way to read.

Knowing Where to Begin

I needed to find a way to build on Maria's strengths to help with her reading difficulties. I pondered the questions, how can I get Maria to actively engage in the reading process? And, what practices could I use to help her think about her own use of strategies in her reading? During the next few weeks I closely observed Maria in class and noted any reading strengths and challenges. I wanted to note all of Maria's reading behaviors in order to find ways to enhance instruction. I used the following assessments:

- Motivation to Read Profile (Gambrell, Palmer, Codling, & Mazzoni, 1999)
- Teachers College Running Record (The Reading and Writing Project, 2004)
- Teacher-student reading conferences

Results from the Motivation to Read Profile

The Motivation to Read Profile consists of 20 items to assess students' motivation to read in two areas: Self-Concept as a Reader and the Value of Reading.

I gave this assessment to Maria by reading the profile out loud to ensure that I would be assessing her motivation to read and not her reading ability. Maria was asked many questions related to her feelings about reading. My observations of Maria since the start of the school year had been correct: Maria wanted her friends to believe she was a good reader, but she didn't think she was a good reader when compared to them. Below are two questions that Maria was asked. Included are two of her responses, about her own reading abilities.

> *Question: My Friends think I am* _____.
>
> *Maria's Response: A very good reader*
>
> *Question: I read* _____.
>
> *Maria's Response : Not as good as my friends.*

The profile showed that Maria had a low self-concept of herself as a reader but a good understanding of the importance or value of reading. Under the sub-scale, Self-Concept as a Reader, Maria scored a 27 out of 40, whereas for the Value of Reading subscale, she scored a 34 out of 40.

Results from Teachers College Running Record

The Teachers College Running Record assessment is used by our school to find a student's approximate independent and instructional reading levels. This is determined by the student orally reading a passage and demonstrating comprehension through a retelling and comprehension questions. After administering the running record and comprehension assessments I was able to note that Maria was below grade level in her reading ability. Her decoding and oral reading skills were on a fourth-grade level, but her comprehension was below grade level. I noticed that Maria was not using any meaning-focused strategies while reading or comprehending the story. For example, Maria did not self-correct herself when reading aloud. If she came to a word she did not know, she often substituted the word with a word that started with the same letter, but didn't make sense in the text. She also showed limited comprehension after reading. One of the comprehension questions asked about a passage from the story *Sounder*, by William H. Armstrong, was "What problem was the boy facing?" Maria gave a very literal response in saying that the boy found a stray dog. She was unable to infer that the dog was abused and the boy didn't want the dog to go back to his owner. I noted that Maria's comprehension was strictly based on literal facts from the story and she found it hard to infer meaning from the events. I needed to help her learn and use strategies effectively to help her understand and enjoy a story and its involved plot. I wanted Maria to become more meta-cognitive as a reader.

Teacher-Student Reading Conferences

During the many conferences with Maria I was able to develop a trust where she felt more comfortable talking about her difficulties as a reader. During one conference, I asked Maria what she thought was hindering her comprehension. Maria responded, "When I am reading I get bored and my mind wonders, I never know what's happening." I asked Maria if she used any strategies when this happened to get her mind back into the story. Maria responded, "No, I don't know any." Maria was able to decode the words but did little to encode the meaning of the text.

 ## Literacy Challenges: Learner and Teacher

My assessments told me that Maria needed help in selecting texts that were appropriate to her reading level. I wanted her to select books based on personal interests and not books that looked impressive to read. In addition, in order to help her advance as a reader and read more challenging books, I needed to help her learn comprehension strategies. During the next few weeks I worked with Maria on selecting appropriate books and on modeling and practicing comprehension strategies that I thought might benefit her.

Selecting Just-Right Books

I spent a lot of time with Maria at our classroom library trying to help her pick a book that she might be interested in and could read with little difficulty. My library is split up into two parts. One half of the library is leveled using the A–Z system developed by Fountas and Pinnell (2001). The books are in baskets labeled with the letter level on front. I would try to point Maria in the right direction of about two to three baskets (Levels M, N and O). Beginning fourth-grade levels are O and P. By this time in the school year, on-grade readers are reading books on levels P and Q. I tried giving exciting book talks to recommend some chapter books that were appropriate to Maria's reading level. I was quickly disappointed as I continued to observe Maria looking around the room rather than at her independent reading book. I even thought Maria might not like the books in our library and invited her to look in other fourth-grade classrooms, which were also leveled in the same way. Each time Maria came back with either no book, or a book with 500 pages, above her reading level (S and higher). We even spent a few minutes together looking through a book order form to pick out some books that she would be interested in. Nothing seemed to work. She would switch from book to book, without finishing one. Ironically, although Maria would never read independently in class, when it was time to go outside to play after lunch, she would ask if she could bring her book outside to read. She thought it was cool to have a big book and to show how she was reading to both the teacher and her classmates.

Modeling Comprehension Strategies

I thought that perhaps Maria was not paying attention during whole-class mini-lessons and that if I modeled strategy use (Pressley, 2002) in one-on-one conferences and during guided reading groups, she would better understand the strategies and begin using them more effectively. For example, during a guided reading group, which provides small group instruction where the teacher can focus on a common need of the students, I modeled the strategy of questioning the text. Before the students started reading their guided reading book, I questioned the group about the strategy.

> **Ms. Agnetti:**   Who can remind us what questioning the text means?
>
> **Maria:**   (raising her hand eagerly) When we ask a question about the story?
>
> **Ms. Agnetti:**   Good, and why would we do this, Maria?
>
> **Maria:**   Umm . . . to come up with good questions.

Maria didn't see questioning the text as a strategy that would promote comprehension but rather as a strategy that in her words would help come up with good questions. At the beginning of our guided reading session, I shared aloud the questions that I had in my head when reading the text. The questions I asked were related to a character in the book to show how questioning should relate to specific events or characters in the story, to help the reader search for answers. While the group continued to read the book quietly, I had to ask Maria to focus on her book several times. She was not actively engaged and was often looking around the room or at the other readers in the group. After we finished the book, I asked each student how they used today's strategy while reading. Maria responded, "Yes, I wondered if I was going to like the book." Maria's question was general and was not a question that improved her comprehension. She was not able to make a connection to a specific event or character in the story. Guided reading groups were not helping me reach Maria's needs as a learner. Her comprehension was not improving, and I felt as though I needed to continue to experiment with ideas, knowing that the right combination of practices would eventually lead to her reading improvement.

Explicit Instruction Is Not Effective by Itself

As I entered my third year using a balanced literacy approach, I thought I had a good grasp of the literacy workshop model I used in my classroom. However, I soon found that I was still unclear on how to motivate some children to want to read and to be aware of their own reading processes. I was implementing guided reading and conferencing with my students daily, but found that something was missing. No matter how hard I tried to spark an interest in reading and strategy use in my students, it was evident that it was not working for all of them. Students such as Maria needed an internal motivation for their learning. Maria's reading improvement needed to have a purpose or a function in her life. It was evident that guided reading, mini-lessons, and conferences, as well as teacher and parent positive reinforcement, were not enough for her to want to work toward becoming a better reader. I needed to consider an approach that would give Maria an opportunity to see a real and personal purpose for reading.

 ## Addressing the Challenge

A solution finally came to me, and delivered by Maria! One Friday, Maria approached me to ask if our class would be going to Reading Buddies that afternoon. Reading Buddies was a program in our school where the upper-grade students read to younger grade students for one period a week. At the time my fourth-grade class was paired with a kindergarten class. My students looked forward to their weekly meetings with the kindergartners. The day that Reading Buddies was canceled because we were going on a class trip, my students moaned with disappointment. I noticed that, like many other students, when Friday afternoon came Maria would ask, "What time are we going to Reading Buddies?" It was her chance to shine as a reader. She was excited to read to her buddy and felt confident in her skills while interacting with a younger student.

I wondered how this program could be modified to help benefit students such as Maria: those who were good decoders but lacked comprehension and purpose for their reading. I knew I needed to give Maria a more genuine purpose for reading and to provide a situation that would help her gain the confidence she needed while reflecting on her own use of reading strategies. I wondered whether Reading Buddies could somehow help Maria and other students to become more active in their reading.

Cross-Age Tutoring

I decided to do some research to see what other teachers have done, beyond having learners read books to their younger peers. I learned that some educators have found benefits in cross-age tutoring (Brewer, Reid, & Rhine, 2003; Labbo & Teale, 1990), and decided on modifying the Reading Buddy program to a cross-age tutoring program. In addition to my students reading to their buddies, I wanted to have my fourth-grade students plan and teach a lesson on a helpful reading strategy to tutor their younger buddies. I arranged to pair my class up with a second-grade class after our winter break, because the second-grade students were learning some of the same strategies that we were learning in fourth grade, but on a simpler level. The second-grade teacher and I collaborated and decided that the fourth-grade tutors would teach the strategies of making connections, questioning, and visualizing (Harvey & Goudvis, 2000). We also decided that the sessions would take place on Friday afternoons, giving the tutors time to design and practice their lesson plans throughout the week. I hoped that if the fourth-grade students were invited to take on the role of tutor, they would accept the responsibility and see a purpose for learning and teaching the reading strategies.

Because this was a new idea, I decided to implement the tutoring model with only five of my students, than my entire class. I chose Maria and four of my other fourth-grade students, who I believed could also benefit from this special focus. Although my whole class of 34 participated in the buddy reading program, these five students were assigned a more defined role as tutors. I met with the five students to explain the new program and their role as tutors. At first Maria seemed concerned about this new opportunity, quickly asking how old the students would be. I explained that the students would be in second grade, and I noticed that Maria's concern faded into a smile. All the students appeared to be excited about the program and quickly began to ask many questions about what they would be teaching. I continued our discussion by introducing the lesson plan sheet. I even introduced a professional teaching book to the students and explained that teachers get ideas from everywhere on how to plan their lessons. At first one of the tutors responded with, "That's a teacher's book, we can't read that." Later in the program that same student asked to borrow my "professional book," because he wanted some suggestions on teaching his second grader the strategy of visualization. I went on to discuss how we would meet as a group to help each other plan the lessons. All the students seemed ready and focused on their new role as tutors.

Days later, Maria's mother approached me in the school yard. She shared, "Maria is so excited about this Reading Buddy thing, she came home yesterday telling everyone she was a reading teacher." She continued to tell me how Maria practiced teaching reading to her younger cousin using a blackboard, and told her mother she needed to get ready for Reading Buddies.

I was starting to see other ways in which Maria was taking an interest as a Reading Buddies tutor. In one of our reading conferences, I asked her about her readiness for our new Reading Buddies experience. The conversation showed how serious she was about her tutoring.

Ms. Agnetti: Maria, I heard you have been practicing your tutoring at home with your cousin. So you're getting ready for Reading Buddies?

Maria: Yeah, I have been going over some lessons with my baby cousin, I teach the strategies I am going to teach my buddy.

Ms. Agnetti: That's great. So which did you teach?

Maria: Connections, but I wasn't sure how to teach it.

Ms. Agnetti: Well, during our next tutoring meeting maybe some of the tutors could help. We can even read some of the questionnaires and see how other teachers teach it.

Maria: OK.

For the first time I noticed that Maria was verbalizing her need for assistance. Her new job as tutor gave her a reason to ask for assistance and a need to understand the strategies.

Being a Reading Teacher

During the first session, Maria introduced herself to her buddy Jen and talked about what the program was. They read a short picture book in order to become familiar with one another. As I observed the students I noticed enthusiasm in both students. Maria seemed to have a new sense of confidence while communicating with her buddy, whereas Jen seemed mesmerized by her fourth-grade tutor. At the end of the session, Maria came to me and said, "That was fun. She needs some help with her reading, but I know I'll help her." I found it amazing that this second-grade student's need for reading assistance was helping Maria become more enthusiastic and motivated about reading.

Each week Maria and four other students met with me to prepare a lesson for their buddies. Monday mornings was the designated time for our weekly tutor meetings. The tutors and I met on the rug to discuss what strategy they would teach and to collaborate on lesson plan ideas. I designed a lesson plan template for the tutors to plan and record: the book selected for their sessions, the strategies they would model, and questions to ask their buddies to assess understanding of the story. The tutors prepared their lesson on Monday morning, reviewed it during the week, and implemented it Friday afternoon during Reading Buddies.

As this routine continued over a 5-month period, I began to notice many positive changes in Maria, as well as the other students involved. The Reading Buddy program was motivating students to self-monitor their reading and verbalize their strategy use (Pressley, 2002). When the students were given the responsibility to fully understand a strategy in order to teach, they showed signs that they were able to reflect on their cognitive processes. The following is from a taped conversation between Maria and her buddy Jen during Reading Buddies. Notice the change in Maria's understanding of the strategy of asking questions, as she teaches Jen the strategy during their reading of the book *Pinduli* (Cannon, 2004).

My Plan	Evaluation	Rubric Rating
Strategy I will teach	Did you think the student learned how to use the strategy? (explain)	
Book I will use	Was the book appropriate and useful in teaching the strategy? (explain)	
How I will model the strategy	Did you model the strategy in an effective way so the second grade student could understand how it is used?	
Questions I will ask to assess student understanding	Did you come up with good questions that encouraged accountable talk?	

Overall, how do you think the session went?

_____

MARIA: OK, today you are going to learn how to come up with good questions when you are reading a story. Watch as I read the story and write down on a sticky note a question I have about the story. (Maria reads the book, then stops to model the strategy.)

MARIA: (Puts her thumb up) I have a question about this part when I was reading it. I was thinking . . . I wonder why the dog is making fun of Pinduli. (Maria writes the question on the sticky note and puts in on the page.)

MARIA: Now, as I read I am going to try and find the answer to that question I have in my mind. Now, I want you to try to do the same thing. When I am reading, if you have a connection give me thumbs up when you have a question and we will stop and write it down on a sticky note.

JEN: (Jen gives her a thumbs up.) I wonder if they [Dog, Lion, Zebra] are going to be nice to Pinduli at the end of the book. (Maria gives Jen a sticky note and Jen writes her question down.)

MARIA: Good question. Let's keep reading to see if we can find the answers to our questions. (Together, they finished the book and discussed the two questions that they came up with while reading. They revisited the parts in the book that answered their questions.)

At the end of the book Maria went on to assess her buddy's understanding through questioning.

MARIA: So Jen, what strategy did I teach you today?

JEN: Questions.

MARIA: Good, remember you want to come up with questions so that when you are reading you are trying to think about answers to the questions.

I was thrilled by Maria's growth in being able to understand how strategies help the reading process and to help her buddy understand its importance. I also saw evidence of this in her participation during our tutor meetings. On one particular occasion, the students were asked if they felt the tutoring sessions were helping them in their own reading. The students had many different responses about the effect Reading Buddies has had on their own reading.

JARED: Until Reading Buddies I never really thought about the strategies. Now, I have been thinking about the strategies more and which strategies I use the most.

JOE: I always knew I used some strategies when I read, but now I am able to notice what specific strategies.

MARIA: When my buddy asks me questions about the strategy it makes me think about the strategy so I could explain it to her. I start to think about how and when I use it.

These comments showed me that the tutors were thinking about the strategies in order to reach their goal of being effective tutors.

As the tutor meetings continued I noticed that Maria was getting very comfortable with asking for assistance or clarification from her peers. During one meeting Maria and her fellow tutors discussed the strategy of making connections to their reading. During this conversation I noticed that Maria's understanding of the strategy, as well as how it is used, was enhanced from her fellow tutors' explanations.

MARIA: Last week's session didn't go so well. I think it was the book I choose, it wasn't a good book to use for connections. Plus, my buddy made a connection and talked about the connection and forgot about the rest of the book.

JARED: I used the book *Pinduli* and it was perfect because it had many second-grade situations, which made it easy for a second grader to practice making connections.

JOE: Maria, what you need to do is make sure that you explain to your buddy that they shouldn't stop reading and make a connection, if you think about, it should just happen, that's how I make connections when I'm reading.

Maria showed signs of evaluating her lesson plan and her thinking behind it. By noticing comprehension problems in others, Maria and her fellow tutors were becoming reflective on their uses of the strategies in their own reading lives. They were helping each other use higher cognitive thinking skills to find ways to improve their lessons. The session brought to Maria's attention the importance of using the strategy of connections in a natural way. Joe was reflective about his use of the strategy to find an effective way to reach the second-grade students. I noticed how focused the tutors were on identifying problems their buddies were having. By doing this, they were thinking about their use of the strategy in order to rethink the choices they made for their buddies.

I began to observe that Maria's own comprehension was improving. I noted during our independent conferences Maria's frequent use of the reading strategies that she was teaching her buddy. Maria was not only teaching her buddy a specific strategy; she was teaching herself how to use it effectively. In her desire to become a successful tutor, she was finding the knowledge she needed about the strategies to construct meaning in her own reading life. Here is one of our later conferences that year.

MS. AGNETTI: So how's it going with your book?

MARIA: Good.

MS. AGNETTI: So what's it about?

MARIA: About a fifth-grade class who has an election for class president.

MS. AGNETTI: Do you like the book?

MARIA: Yes, it's interesting.

MS. AGNETTI: So what made you pick this book?

MARIA: I read the first few pages and it seemed like a good book.

MS. AGNETTI: It sounds like a really cool book. Can you read a little to me and maybe we can discuss what is going on?

(Maria read two pages. I noticed that her fluency was very good and she was reading with expression. I stopped her and asked if she could summarize what she just read.)

MARIA: Well, these two boys both want to run for president and they are trying to win by making banners and posters and hanging them all over the school. They both have their friends helping them make a campaign so they could win

Ms. Agnetti: Wow, you really got what was happening in this part of the book. Did you use any strategies while you were reading, like questioning or connections?

Maria: Well, I was thinking about how in the beginning of the year we had a class election to pick a class flag.

Ms. Agnetti: I started to think about that too.

Maria: Yeah, it was like we did the same things as the characters—remember we made the flags and made posters to get people in the school to vote for our flag?

Ms. Agnetti: Yeah, wow, that was a good connection. I always do that when I am reading, I make connections to the text. Isn't that what you taught your reading buddy last week?

Maria: Yeah.

Ms. Agnetti: Did she understand it?

Maria: Well, sort of. She would make connections and go off on the topic of her connection. This week I am going to explain that she can't do that. She needs to let the connection just happen so she can picture what's happening in the book.

Ms. Agnetti: What do you mean? I'm a little confused.

Maria: Like when I was reading I didn't stop and start talking about our class election, but when I read that part about the posters, I was thinking also about when we made posters like that in our class. It helped me think about what was happening.

Ms. Agnetti: Wow, that's really smart.

Maria: Yeah, I talked about it with Joe and he helped me with connections.

Maria was also using the tutor meetings to find answers to questions she had about the strategies. I realized that Maria now had the responsibility to teach her second-grade buddy the strategy and therefore she was working hard to feel like an expert at using the strategy in her own reading. Maria was gaining a better understanding of the strategies and was finally using them effectively. It was obvious that her comprehension was improving and she was feeling more confident in her reading abilities. Although Maria would never choose lower level books for herself, the Reading Buddy program was having her choose them for her second-grade buddy. I realized that by choosing a book that she felt was appropriate for her buddy, she was also choosing a book that she was able to read and comprehend. She was gaining confidence in her own abilities, without having to feel embarrassed about her book choices among her fourth-grade peers. She would browse through our classroom library and ask about certain lower level books. Maria was always looking for a book that she felt her buddy would be interested in. She loved to practice reading these books on her own to decide which ones she thought would be good to use for her sessions.

Using Self-Evaluation Forms

While trying to find a way to promote Maria's meta-cognition, her awareness of her thinking process as she makes meaning of texts (Pressley, 2002), I decided to incorporate a self-reflection component to the cross-age tutoring session. Incorporated into each lesson plan were some questions that asked tutors to reflect on each lesson taught and evaluate the outcome of the session. Maria would give each component of the lesson a grade using a rubric based on a 1–4 rating scale. Maria along with the other tutors took time after each session to fill out the self-reflection part of their lesson.

1	Both students are distracted and the strategy is not being verbalized. Conversation is not focused on the strategy.
2	One of the students is focused and the other is not. Conversation during session is OK.
3	Both students are focused and working on the strategy. Good conversation on the topic.
4	Both students are focused and verbalizing the use of the strategy. Conversation is great; students are discussing the reading strategy.

During Maria's first self-reflection, I found it amazing that her perspective on how the session went matched mine. She gave the session an overall grade of 2, noting that she did not pick an appropriate book and her modeling of the strategy was not good. When I conferenced with Maria and asked her about the session, she explained why she felt the second-grade student was unable to understand the strategy. During the conference I noted that Maria was focused on my explanation of the strategy and was eager to understand it herself. She asked many questions that showed her need for clarification on how to use the strategy herself, in order for her to plan a more successful lesson for her upcoming tutoring sessions. Maria and her fellow tutors discussed their evaluation forms at the tutor meetings to help plan better lessons. Maria continued to evaluate her sessions throughout the program, making changes to each lesson based on her evaluation from the week before. She would suggest books to her fellow tutors that she felt were suited to certain strategies. Maria would also ask for suggestions from her peers on ways to plan effective strategy lessons. During the tutor meetings I noted that the tutors were collaborating with one another, which was allowing them to reflect on their own cognitive processes. I also noted how they would discuss and model their own use of the strategy to help a fellow tutor understand the strategy.

After reviewing Maria's lessons and evaluation sheets, I noted that she was beginning to feel that she was more effective. On one evaluation sheet, Maria wrote that the reason she felt the session didn't go well was because she didn't really understand the strategy enough to teach it. During the next tutor meeting I observed Maria asking the other tutors for clarification of this strategy. Maria would continue to ask for assistance and practice modeling the strategy before she would conduct her cross-age tutoring session on Friday afternoons.

As the sessions continued, all the students were becoming better at incorporating effective modeling strategies into their lessons. The tutors started to use sticky notes in their teaching and were learning how to reflect on their ideas and find more effective modeling techniques. I also noticed an increase in the quality of their written self-reflections. In the beginning the tutors responded with short statements such as, "Yes, I modeled effectively." As the program continued they provided actual examples to back up their evaluations. Below are some of Maria's responses to her self-evaluation over time.

Evaluation	**Did you model the strategy in an effective way so the second grade student could understand how it is used?**	**Did you come up with good questions that encouraged accountable talk?**
Reflection 1	*No, I didn't*	*Not really*
Reflection 2	*Yes*	*My questions were o.k. I forgot to ask why do we make connections.*
Reflection 3	*Yes, I modeled using sticky notes and then had Jen use sticky notes too.*	*Yes, I had Jen tell me when and why we make connections to a book. She even told that making connections to a book is when you think about something in your own life that reminds you of the story.*

Learning from Students' Learning

At the start of this experience with the tutors, I found myself wanting to lead than facilitate. I would catch myself wanting to tell Maria that her book choice was not appropriate for the strategy, or that her modeling needed more depth. I refrained and instead took a step back and noticed that through the tutors collaborating, along with conferences and self-evaluation prompts, Maria was discovering her own path to the knowledge she needed to improve as a reader. I also noticed that along the way her confidence not only as a reader but as a learner was improving. Reading Buddies was giving Maria a reason to search for answers to her problems and learn about the reading process. She would ask her fellow tutors for assistance and would practice the strategy during independent reading as well as at home. I couldn't believe that Maria, a student whom I felt I could not motivate to read, was taking her own time at home to practice strategy use in her reading. She felt important and in control of her learning, and this was helping her improve as a student. As I watched Maria and the other students in the group, I realized how important it is to give students space to grapple with their learning and to understand that they need a chance to make a strategy their own, not just to parrot the strategy that I modeled.

Fitting Instruction to Meet the Needs of the Child

Maria came to fourth grade thinking that good readers are those who can read chapter books with small print and lots of pages. She tried to imitate what other strong readers were doing around her—choosing and trying to read books like *Harry Potter*—but didn't seem to get that there was more to reading than turning pages. In the classroom, she aimed to please by trying to parrot the strategy procedures I taught during whole-class lessons, but again without any meaningful purpose. Reading Buddies redirected her purpose for reading and for participating in a learning community with her peer tutors.

Shifting the Goal of Instruction for Maria

For many of my students, revealing the thinking process of what readers do through modeling, thinking aloud, and strategy instruction is the key to helping them take off as meaningful readers. For Maria and a few of my other learners, telling them that reading strategies would help them enjoy a book was not enough. Maria didn't see a purpose for learning a strategy, but Maria did find a purpose in helping younger kids read. Giving Maria the opportunity to tutor a second grader in becoming a strategic reader gave her a reason to learn about the reading process.

Group Meetings Provide a Nurturing Learning Community

The students whom I selected as tutors were heterogeneous in their reading abilities, but shared a common skepticism about learning strategies. Together they began to see the value in understanding reading strategies by being asked to help a second grader. Our time together to plan and give support became a special time for us to think about how we learned and why. Maria was no longer concerned about impressing others as a reader, because they came together to help the second graders and to admit that teaching is tricky and requires thinking. The weekly tutor meetings gave the students a chance to discuss their tutoring sessions and collaborate on new approaches. They were in control of what they wanted to talk about. This opportunity gave Maria the chance to see that reading doesn't come easy for everyone, and that it requires work. The experience also made me think about my own teaching and the importance of giving my students the opportunity to talk about the process and to be flexible in how we use strategies and think about texts.

The process of recognizing and meeting Maria's needs as a learner was one that took time and risk as a teacher. Because many students benefited, the Reading Buddy program was the right combination for Maria, to improve her reading confidence and give her purpose, as well as improve her overall comprehension. As her teacher I had needed to find a way to reach her. It wasn't until I really listened to what Maria did value that I came up with a way to reach her. By really keying into Maria as an individual, I was finally able to give her a purpose for reading and thinking about her learning.

References

Brewer, R., Reid, M., & Rhine, B. (2003). Peer coaching: Students teaching to learn, *Intervention in School and Clinic*, *39*(2), 113–126.

Cannon, J. (2004). *Pinduli*. New York: Harcourt Children's Books.

Fountas, I. C., & Pinnell, G. S. (2001). *Guiding readers and writers grades 3–6*. Portsmouth, NH: Heinemann.

Gambrell, L. B., Palmer, B., Codling, R., & Mazzoni, S. (1999). Assessing motivation to read, In S. J. Barrentine (Ed.), *Reading assessment: Principles and practices for elementary teachers* (pp. 215–231). Newark, DE: International Reading Association.

Harvey, S., & Goudvis, A. (2000). *Strategies that work*. Portland, ME: Stenhouse.

Labbo, L. D., & Teale, W. (1990). Cross-age reading: A strategy for helping poor readers. *The Reading Teacher*, *43*(6), 90–95.

Pressley, M. (2002). Metacognition and self-regulated comprehension. In A. E. Farstrup & S. Samuels (Eds.), *What research has to say about reading instruction* (pp. 291–309). Newark, DE: International Reading Association.

The Reading and Writing Project Teachers College (2004, February) 6–9 Quick Reading Assessment, Columbia University.

Rowling, J. K. (2000). *Harry Potter and the Goblet of Fire*. New York: Scholastic.

6 | Reading for Meaning

Teaching a Fifth Grader to Make Sense of Texts
Through Reciprocal Teaching

Patricia Isoldi, Fifth-Grade Teacher

"I don't understand. I thought I could read!"
Fifth Grader, Rosa

Rosa was a welcome member of my fifth grade inclusion classroom. She was kind, energetic, and funny, and she worked very hard. It was because of these qualities that she stayed "under the radar" for quite some time. I spent much of the beginning of the school year addressing other students in the classroom with significant delays or working with those students who had difficulty with adjusting to a new school year. I also concentrated on establishing routines and creating an environment that encouraged learning. One afternoon during independent reading, Rosa and I conferenced about her self-selected book. I was recording an informal running record and asking her basic comprehension questions, such as who were the significant characters in the story and what had happened in the story so far. Rosa orally read her book well, but my questions changed her mood from the confident reader to silence, and then quiet tears. When I asked her what was wrong, she muttered, "I don't understand!"

When she calmed down, Rosa and I spoke about what she thought was so difficult about the reading. She stated that she did not "get stuck" on any words. However, when it was time to answer questions following the reading, she could not remember what she had read. She tried to answer the questions but couldn't. There were even times when she could not remember the characters' names. Rosa's frustration was clear when she said, "I don't understand. I thought I could read!"

 ## The First Hurdle: Reading Is More Than Decoding Words

I started to watch Rosa more carefully in the classroom. I noticed that she would choose to partner-read with students who read at lower levels. She enjoyed helping these students decode difficult words. During the more challenging parts of reader's workshop, Rosa would work hard to act the part of a "good student." For example, I noticed that during our class discussions of books, Rosa would often repeat the answers given by the strong readers. Our compliments to other students were a cue of sorts for her. If our reactions to a student's comment were positive, she would raise her hand and repeat the comment.

I also spoke with Rosa's mother by telephone. She was reluctant to admit that Rosa had trouble reading. She stated that she sat with Rosa every night and listened to her read. She shared that Rosa liked to borrow difficult books from the library and was able to read these to her. When I inquired about Rosa's understanding of the books she read, her mother replied, "She reads." I tried to explain to Rosa's mother that reading was not simply reading words. Decoding is only one part of the reading process. We also needed to help Rosa make sense of what she read.

 ## Knowing Where to Begin

In order to address Rosa's needs I used a variety of assessments to measure her comprehension. These included:

- Oral reading and comprehension assessments: Developmental Reading Assessment (Beaver, 1997) and assessment materials from Teachers College Reading & Writing Project (2004)
- Written responses to literature
- Reading conferences and classroom observation

Results from Reading Assessments

According to the Developmental Reading Assessment (DRA), Rosa read on a level 34. This level is comparable to our school's leveling system level O (Fountas & Pinnell, 2001), which is a late third-grade text. The text she read for the DRA assessment was *Summer Discovery*, a story about a little boy, Noah, who likes to collect rocks. He is very excited because it is summer vacation and he plans on working on his rock collection and finding a piece of peacock ore. Unfortunately, he finds out that he must spend his summer with his grandparents. He is very angry and sad. He spends the beginning of the summer missing his home and his mom despite the fact that his grandparents go out of their way to cheer him up. To help him adjust, Noah's mom sends him the rock collection. Gramps sees Noah's rock collection and takes a box from the attic. It contains the rock collection he started when he was Noah's age. Noah finds the peacock ore in Gramps's collection and decides that maybe the summer won't be so bad after all.

Rosa read this with 98% accuracy. Her substitutions made sense inside the context of the reading passage. For example, Rosa read "Miss Peck" instead of "Mrs. Peck," and "My dad would *not* have worn a sweater like this" instead of

"My dad would *never* have worn a sweater like this." She repeated the phrase "into his backpack." Her phrasing and fluency were adequate. She read in longer phrases most of the time at an adequate rate, she adjusted intonation to convey meaning, and she attended to punctuation. She displayed no observable behaviors at difficult points of the story, did not appeal for help, and did not detect any miscues, although her few miscues did not affect the meaning of the story.

However, Rosa's comprehension score was 16. Sixteen is the minimum score a child can receive for "adequate comprehension." This was mainly due to Rosa needing more than six prompts to retell the story. Some of the prompts I gave her were:

- Tell me more about . . .
- What happened after . . .?
- Who else was in the story?
- How was Noah's problem solved?
- How did the story end?
- What happened before Gramps gave Noah his father's books?

Rosa had great difficulty determining what was important to retell. Even with prompting, she left out many important events from the story. The events that were retold were not given in sequential order and the events were changed slightly from what was written in the story. Instead of recognizing the importance of Noah going to stay with his grandparents for the summer, Rosa said, "Noah is going to play with Jake." At the end of the story, Noah realizes that Gramps also collected rocks and he begins to think that the summer will not be so boring after all. He begins to enjoy his grandfather's company and looks forward to spending time with him. Rosa missed the impact of the rock collection on Noah and Gramps's relationship and said, "At the end, Noah gets to collect more rocks."

I decided to use a second reading assessment to compare results. My reading coach suggested the Teachers College Reading Assessment (The Reading and Writing Project; Teachers College, 2004) because it consists of a short excerpt taken from actual children's literature and has fewer follow-up questions. I administered the Level O assessment, *Ramona Forever*, by Beverly Cleary. In this excerpt from the book *Ramona Forever*, Ramona is visiting Willa Jean Kemp. Willa Jean received an accordion from her Uncle Hobart as a gift. Willa Jean does not know how to play the accordion and gets frustrated. She tries to play it, then steps on it and sits on it. Finally, the accordion emits a terrible, loud sound and breaks. Willa Jean's mother responds to the commotion. She blames Ramona for the broken accordion, because Ramona is older than Willa Jean and was therefore responsible. Rosa's performance was similar to her performance on the DRA. She read with 100% accuracy and was fluent. Her retell showed literal ideas with some inaccuracies,

Throughout the retell she referred to Ramona as "he" instead of "she." She also thought that Ramona received the accordion as a gift from her grandfather.

> Ramona got an accordion from his grandfather. He was learning how to play it and put his feet in the straps. His cousin Willa Jean wanted to play it but she broke it.
> Ramona got in trouble because he was supposed to watch Willa Jean but he didn't and Willa Jean broke the accordion. Ramona got in trouble. Willa Jean said it was just a dumb old accordion and it wouldn't play.

Rosa's Retelling of *Ramona Forever* (Cleary, 1990).

In fact, the accordion was a gift to Willa Jean from her uncle. Rosa's retelling was clearly missing many key elements and did not match the story. She showed little evidence of making any interpretations of the incident.

Rosa's Written Responses to Literature

Rosa's written responses to literature were lengthy as she made sure to fill entire sheets of loose leaf. These responses looked great. But like her oral retellings, Rosa's ideas were very scattered, often lacked accuracy, and did not go beyond literal events.

This is evident in Rosa's response to *Henry Huggins*, by Beverly Cleary. *Henry Huggins* is about a third grader named Henry. Henry is very upset because he feels nothing exciting ever happens to him. One day, while in a drugstore, Henry meets a stray dog. The dog takes Henry's ice cream and "ate it in one gulp." Henry decides to name the dog Ribsy and take him home. Henry's life immediately changes. Rosa wrote:

> Henry found a big dog. Henry couldn't take the bus to go home unless it's in a box. When Ribsy and Henry got on the bus Ribsy came out of the bag and the people on the bus dropped stuff. Henry bought guppies. There were also baby guppies in the bowl. Henry didn't have enough space to put his guppies in his room. Henry has to get rid of guppies. Scooter's football fell into a car that passed by Henry and Scooter. Henry had to recite in front of adults. Henry was a little boy in a play and he had to get kissed by a girl playing his mom. Henry feels embaresed because he gets kissed by a eight grader girl. Henry feels annoyed about kids calling him Timmy/name of boy in play.

Rosa's reading response for *Henry Huggins* (Cleary, 1990).

There is no link between ideas, and there does not seem to be any connection within the events. She does not seem to understand that the big moments in a book must connect to form even bigger plot ideas.

I also noticed that Rosa's responses did not show improvement after my explicit teaching of a particular literacy focus. At this time our mini-lessons focused on the importance of taking a closer look at the setting of a book. In my read-alouds prior to independent reading time, I modeled how readers pay attention to setting as they read. These modeling sessions lasted 4 days. I shared with students how different authors use a variety of ways to describe a setting to create the mood in a story. After presenting models, I invited students to share their thoughts and ideas in conversations about what they noticed about an author's descriptions of place and time, and how each description helped to create the book's mood. When the students had enough exposure, I asked them to "have a go" during their independent reading to notice how the author of their self-selected books described setting and created a mood in the story. Rosa's response to her book, *No Flying in the House* by Betty Brock, focused on the book's setting; however, she did not describe the setting beyond physical location to address the story's mood. She wrote,

> In the books setting I noticed that Mrs. Vancourt live in a house that has gardens around it. Mrs. Vancourt lives in Europe. You can over look a sea from Mrs. Vancourts house. Mrs. Vancourt has an immense house. That is what I noticed about my books setting.
>
> Rosa's reading response for *No Flying in the House* (Brock, 1982).

Rosa also had difficulty responding to nonfiction texts. After reading a narrative passage from *National Geographic Explorer* about cowboy Nat Love (from "Forgotton Cowboys" by Brian LaFleur), she was asked to agree or disagree with the author as to whether or not Nat Love was one of the greatest cowboys ever. She was able to pull details out of the text; however, these details were not always relevant to the text and she did not write a clear response.

> I agree with the author that Nat Love was one of the greatest cowboys ever. I agree because Nat didn't have an education and he actually got a job. Nat Love became very population. As a cowboy Nat made $30.00 an hour. Most people thought that all cowboys were white. But Nat Love was one of the African American cowboys. The fact that Nat was African American and people thought cowboys were white I think it's special that he's one of the African American cowboys.

The author of the article did state that Nat Love was the greatest cowboy ever; it was not because he was Black. The author did say that it was astonishing that Nat Love became so successful despite the fact that he was Black in a time when that might have seriously held him back. The author states that Nat Love was a great cowboy because of his expertise with rope, horses, and cattle. He could perform tricks and became very popular because of his talents, not simply because he was a Black cowboy.

Reading Conferences and Classroom Observations

Subsequent reading conferences and classroom literature discussions showed similar results. Rosa read with great accuracy. However, when asked to discuss books, she rarely moved beyond offering literal details of a story. Rosa either repeated the ideas of her peers or responded with sentences from the text, sometimes unrelated to our focus. When she recalled ideas from memory, she often jumbled her facts. Rosa struggled when asked to think deeply about texts.

 ## Literacy Challenges: Learner and Teacher
Restructuring Guided Reading Groups

Rosa's limited comprehension skills made it difficult for her to interpret literal ideas accurately some of the time, and to go beyond the literal text most of the time. This also had a direct effect on her writing. She had limited ways to discuss the story. When Rosa would read books, she wasn't getting a clear picture. Therefore, when she would try to write about the story, her writing would reflect the confusion in her head. She would reread her writing but did not notice any mistakes because it matched what she had in her head about the story.

I decided to rethink the purpose of my guided reading groups. Instead of basing the grouping strictly on reading levels, the new groups were based on specific reading challenges. I had heard about doing this before, but now I really saw the need for forming such groups. I placed Rosa in a guided reading group of four with other students who were performing on levels O–Q and had difficulties making meaning from texts.

I started by getting the students to realize that they had to read strategically. We began by reviewing different ideas that the students had about reading. We spoke about how effective reading involves using strategies to think about the author's message. We created a list of the strategies that they knew readers do in their head to make sense of texts. Their list included that readers (1) make a movie in their mind, (2) replace words they do not know with words that sound right and make sense, and (3) stop at the end of the page to do a "mini-retell" to make sure they understood what they read. Although they could identify strategies, these four students showed little evidence of applying any of them regularly. I chose to begin by focusing on how a reader might stop to do a "mini-retell" while reading.

We used the story *Suzie Ridinghood* (Macmillan, 2001). It's a story about a small girl who lives in a small town with her mother. Her grandmother also lives in this town in a house that lies on the other side of a path through the woods. Suzie's grandfather helped survey the woods for the pathways and bridges the town wanted to build. Her grandfather's work inspires Suzie and she decides to become a surveyor as well. Fast forward a few years later, and Suzie is now a surveyor—and her small town needs her help. The city wants to run a major highway through the woods that Suzie grew up loving. Suzie must go and survey the land herself to come up with an alternate route for the highway. Suzie saves the day by creating a plan that satisfies everyone's needs and concerns.

I introduced our focus of doing a mini-retelling as a strategy for keeping track when reading. I demonstrated how to jot down a few sentences on a Post-it to summarize the key events that took place on each page. We talked about the importance of stopping to think about what we read so that we can check our understanding, and do something to clear up our confusion before we read on. We then read the story individually and stopped after each page to retell, each student using a Post-it to record his or her ideas. We also created a list of characters in the story and added to it every time we came across a new character. It was my hope this would help the students keep the characters straight in their minds and they would eventually not have to refer to the list.

Rosa's jot for the first page was great. "Suzie is little girl who lives with her mother in a small town. She walks through the woods when she wants to see her grandma." This was the important information the author presented in the first page. As we read further, the pages became longer and there was more information given to the reader than on previous pages. The students had more difficulty writing these jots and most were missing the important information. We read the page where Suzie is on her way to her grandmother's and we learned that Suzie's grandfather helped the woods become usable by the townspeople. This is very important to Suzie and is what leads to her becoming a surveyor herself. The students' jots ranged from "Suzie visits her grandma" to "Suzie really likes walking through the woods." The students were missing the information the author wanted to communicate. The students and I discussed this and decided it would be best to stop after each paragraph for a little while just to make sure they did not miss any important information. This seemed to improve their ability to summarize the big idea in each paragraph.

Too Much Teacher Direction

As we continued to meet as a group, I noticed that Rosa and the others were struggling still. As we read new stories, the students became quiet and hesitant to answer questions. Rosa was volunteering less and less. Our sessions were becoming very teacher directed and the students did not seem to be improving. The atmosphere was becoming very formal. I would ask a question and they would raise their hands and answer it. No one offered any ideas or insights other than those that related to my questions. When questions required them to infer anything beyond a simple prediction, they stared at me, waiting for help. I realized that they were not taking ownership of any strategies. My questioning was partly to blame.

Addressing the Challenge
Reciprocal Teaching Is Introduced

I needed a way to get the students to engage in the active process of reading, so I decided to try reciprocal teaching. Reciprocal teaching is an instructional approach for discussing a text by involving readers in four comprehension strategies: predicting, questioning, clarifying, and summarizing. During reciprocal teaching, the teacher and students take turns acting as the facilitator in guiding a discussion of the text through use of the four strategies (Palincsar & Brown, 1984). According to McLaughlin and Allen (2002), reciprocal teaching is used to help learners to understand that the reading process involves continual use of these four strategies and to become more aware of their learning and thinking processes. In the beginning stages, the teacher models the role of facilitator and demonstrates each of the strategies. As students become more comfortable and familiar with the strategies, they begin to take over as facilitator, receiving as little guidance as possible (Duke & Pearson, 2002). Reciprocal Teaching enables students to activate their own prior knowledge, monitor their own understanding and acquire a deeper understanding of the text (King & Parent Johnson, 1999; Oczkus, 2003).

I began introducing reciprocal teaching with Rosa's guided reading group. Originally, I chose to focus on modeling one strategy at a time. The first chosen was predicting. Prediction was chosen because I thought it to be the most familiar, and thereby the easiest for the students to understand. I began by strictly modeling prediction using the book *A Chair for My Mother* by Vera B. Williams. The students did not seem engaged. They asked why they were only allowed to use prediction. I tried to explain that I wanted them to be able to focus their efforts on one strategy at a time. The students watched me model prediction three separate times and did not seem any more engaged or any closer to understanding the literature. I needed guidance.

I was able to watch *Reciprocal Teaching*, a video by the New Zealand Ministry of Education. It showed a classroom of students engaged in reciprocal teaching. The video portrayed a group of students very smoothly performing reciprocal teaching using expository text. There were about 10–15 students participating and one teacher guiding the process. The students were using all four components during the session. The roles of the students were clearly outlined and the teacher was there for guidance. After seeing this video and discussing what was going on with my students with my school's reading consultant, I decided to take a different approach.

I realized that it did not make sense to model the four components (prediction, questioning, clarifying, and summarizing) in isolation because that is not what we do as readers. When reading, we use our strategies interchangeably, some more often than others, depending on the text. By breaking down reciprocal teaching, I was fostering my students' inclination to isolate strategies. Furthermore, students needed more explicit modeling before I could expect them to take on the strategies themselves. My reading consultant suggested *a minimum* of 12 lessons for explicit modeling. I also decided to teach the lessons to the whole class, not only four students. My co-teacher, a special education teacher, and I discussed what a powerful strategy reciprocal teaching could be and how it might benefit all of our students.

I looked for materials to support my students in taking control of reciprocal teaching discussions. Although I found numerous sources, the materials I found to meet my purposes included a list of student prompts and an RT Checklist on an Internet site from a school district in Newton, Kansas (http://www.newton.k12.ks.us/Dist/curr/bp/lit/reciprocal_teaching.htm). I created a list on large chart paper of the different prompts students could select to help them to think through their reading.

Predicting

- I can look at the title and other visual clues. What do I think I will be reading about?
- Thinking about what I have read and discussed, I think _____ will happen next.
- I wonder . . .
- I predict . . .

Questioning

- One question I have about what I read is . . .
- What were you thinking about while you were reading?
- What questions can we ask about this page?
- I am curious about . . .

Clarifying

- One of the words I wasn't sure about was _____.
- What other words can we use in place of _____?
- What words or ideas do you need clarified?
- This (*page, word, paragraph, section, etc.*) is confusing for me. I need to _____ to figure it out.

Summarizing

- What does the author want me to remember or learn from this page?
- The most important information on this page is . . .
- In my own words, this (*page, paragraph, section, article, etc.*) is about . . .
- What is the main idea of this page?

Each child also received a copy of these prompts on cardstock in plastic sleeves for easy referencing during teaching and group work.

I began whole group modeling using narrative nonfiction articles from *Time for Kids*, Grade 4. I chose these particular texts because the authors write in narrative style, despite the nonfiction content. They are short pieces that often have large, clear photographs to accompany the article. The students took their seats at the meeting area and I used an overhead projector to display the article to the entire class.

The students enjoyed the articles and found it easy to follow my think-alouds with the prompt cards. The photo combined with the title made for very easy predictions, and the succinctness of the article enabled the students to pay attention and not lose focus. I audio recorded the sessions, so that I could critique the lesson and reflect on how I would proceed in the next day's lesson. The students, including Rosa, were all very eager to use the strategies with the prompt cards themselves. They loved the idea that they would take turns being the "teacher"/facilitator. They made observations and offered comments. Rosa's comment was, "I noticed that you looked at the prompt chart a lot." She would later say that she liked the prompt chart because she did not feel so nervous with it. After her comment another child said, "Yeah and you jumped around on the chart a lot. I mean you used all the parts, not just one." In other words, she had noticed that I used prompts from all four strategies of reciprocal teaching.

Through my reflections on my think-alouds for the students, I noticed I was not always addressing the questions I raised about the different vocabulary words with which I claimed to have difficulty. I made a concerted effort to remedy this for the next modeling. I asked the students for some strategies they use when they come across a word they did not know in their reading. Most responded with "putting in a word that sounded right and made sense."

After approximately six modeling sessions, I began giving the students more responsibility during our RT discussions (Duke & Pearson, 2002). Different short texts were put onto overhead sheets and the class gathered at the meeting area. I would act as facilitator, setting up the stopping points to guide predictions and ask the students different questions. The students would notify me at each stopping point if they had a question or a word or idea they did not understand and wanted to clarify. After questions and clarifications (addressed by the students when possible), we tried to summarize the information in the section, always concentrating on calling all characters by their names. After summarizing the text, we created predictions about the next portion of the text. For this guided portion, I read the text on the overhead projector and reminded the students each time to refer to their prompt cards to help them. After three guided sessions, we broke up into small groups. Because the class is an inclusion classroom with collaborative team teaching, my co-teacher and I each rotated among two groups. Each group contained four students. One of those groups was Rosa and three other students who shared similar comprehension challenges. All guided reading groups used reciprocal teaching; however, I focused primarily on Rosa and her group's progress, as she presented the learning challenge that I was most interested in tackling.

We read *Yagua Days* by Cruz Martel. *Yagua Days* is story about a boy, Adan Riera, who lives on the Lower East Side of Manhattan. It is summer vacation and it is raining. The mailman, Jorge, tells Adan that rainy days are wonderful because they are *yagua* days. Jorge grew up in Puerto Rico with Adan's parents and they shared many *yagua* days. Adan and his family then go to Puerto Rico to visit family. It is a bright, sunny day and Adan asks if it is a *yagua* day. His uncle replies that it is the worst because the sun is out. This confuses Adan even more. Eventually Adan does indeed learn what a *yagua* day is and learns to love them just as much as his parents do.

I chose this text because of its intriguing title and references to Puerto Rican culture. The students in the group were all from Puerto Rico or the Dominican Republic. I hoped that the vocabulary and descriptions would help them connect to the story better. It did not have the desired effect. Before we began, prompt cards were handed to each child and I acted as a facilitator. I suggested stopping points where the students pause to predict what would happen in the story. My questions and prompts were greeted with silence. I altered my original plans to let the students take most of the control and again modeled the task. I split *Yagua Days* into two sessions and went through the process slowly with the students to engage them in a conversation about the book. I tried asking them the translations to some of the Spanish, to have them help me clarify my meaning making, and hoping they would connect to the story. I had flashbacks to my previous guided reading group, routine question and answer. No one initiated a discussion with the prompt cards. I thought perhaps the students were using me as a crutch.

Adapting Reciprocal Teaching to Encourage Active Participation

I decided to give them some guidance by assigning each student a specific role for reciprocal teaching discussions and gave each student one of the four strategies to facilitate (McLaughlin & Allen, 2002). I used a checklist to monitor their use of these roles and strategies (see http://www.newton.k12.ks.us/Dist/curr/bp/lit/reciprocal_teaching.htm). I wanted to record how many times students referred to their prompt cards on their own and how many times they had to be reminded. The hope was the students would eventually use the cards automatically and not need them at all. The check-off list also provided an easier way to track progress and record notes during the sessions.

Each seat at the table was designated with a role or strategy. Students rotated each session to have an opportunity to facilitate all strategies. The child holding the prediction role card started the session. In the beginning, I designated the stopping point; later this became the responsibility of the child in the first chair. The Predictor made a prediction based on the title, any headings, or any photographs or illustrations. The student then asked if anyone would like to agree or disagree based on other evidence given or a different interpretation. The students read the allotted amount of text and stopped. Next the Clarifier asked if anyone read any words or phrases that needed to be clarified. Using the prompt cards the students offered up different difficulties and the other three students tried to clarify, by either offering different words to substitute or trying to give the main idea of the sentence despite not knowing the exact definition of the word. It was then the job of the Questioner to ask different questions. Each one must be answered before moving onto the next one. Last, the Summarizer used the prompt card to summarize the text or the important information discussed during conversation. When all these parts were completed, the students read on to the next point and repeated the entire process. At the end of the reading, the students were all required to write a response to the text. Often in the beginning, the responses were simply retellings of the story. However, these retellings were often accurate and more sequential than previous responses.

In our early sessions, Rosa and the other students followed the prompt cards very closely. They had to be reminded to use the cards to keep them on track; otherwise, they would go off on different tangents. Usually, these tangents did not relate to the story. Rosa never spoke out of turn, but always had to be reminded to refer to her prompt card and her role card. She confided in me that she liked being in the first seat because she thought making predictions was easy. When I asked her why she thought it was easy she replied, "Because I only have to make predictions after we talk about the story. I can use other people's ideas to help me. That makes it a lot easier." Rosa was still relying on the ideas of others. I made a note to observe how often she responded to questions and thoughts given by other students and to praise her initiations. I noted that in four sessions, Rosa answered two questions. When I pointed this out to her, she said she felt "silly" because she "didn't want to give the wrong answer in front of everyone." At the next session Rosa had to be reminded what to do and to use her cards five times. When I asked her about this, she said it was because she was "planning out" what she would say during the questioning session.

Over time, our group discussions were becoming just that—discussions. This did not happen until mid-March, approximately 2 months after I began reciprocal teaching sessions and 1 month after I introduced role cards. The child who had taken on the leadership role in the group asked, "Can I ask a question that isn't on the card?" When I replied, "Of course!" the other students seemed surprised. I explained to them that soon they would feel that they no longer needed the prompts and would guide their discussions by their own thinking.

We read *Jamaica Tag Along* by Juanita Havill. The story is about a young girl, Jamaica, and her big brother, Ossie. Ossie makes plans to go to the park and Jamaica wants to go with him. He reluctantly allows her to follow him to the basketball courts. While there, Jamaica makes her way over to the sandlot. She treats a small boy the same way Ossie treats her and realizes that she has hurt the boy's feelings. Jamaica and the boy build a sand castle and become friends. Ossie asks if he can join in and Jamaica "doesn't even mind if Ossie tags along." Rosa initiated the discussion by asking them to share different times when their older siblings treated them as Ossie (since all happened to have an older brother or sister). Rosa said, "We probably can guess how Jamaica feels because it happened to us too. And I disagree with what Karim said. I don't think Ossie is a bad big brother. He probably just got annoyed with Jamaica and wanted to be with his friends. That happens sometimes. I think he felt bad about it too because he went over later and asked if he could build the sand castle with them." This was a huge breakthrough. This comment showed that Rosa read the story, understood the story, was able to keep the characters straight, and connected personally to the book.

Rosa continued to blossom within the group setting. We read the book *A Day's Work* by Eve Bunting. I asked the students to write a reflection about the book stating whether they agreed with Francisco lying to Ben to get Abuelo a job. They also had to write whether Francisco deserved to be paid after they failed to complete the job. Rosa wrote the reflection:

Francisco lied about his grandpa's working skills and Francisco told Ben that his grandpa is a fine gardener. I think that it was wrong for Francisco to lie because his grandpa didn't know how to garden and he used to live in a city in Mexico. Ben might leave Francisco's grandfather alone since he said he is a fine gardener. Francisco's grandfather does not know how to garden so he will get fired. Another reason why it was wrong to lie was because if Francisco told the truth his grandpa would have probably got a job as a carpenter and get more money. This would have helped Francisco and his mom because his mom would need more money for food and she would need more food for grandpa. She will also need money for rent and bills. Some other ideas that I had about this story is that Ben shouldn't pay Francisco and his grandpa because Francisco lied and Ben thought grandpa knew how to garden. Ben also shouldn't pay them because he has to pay someone else to plant the flowers and take out the weeds. If Francisco didn't be like this wouldn't have happened. Grandpa must have been embarrassed. If I was Francisco I would have told Ben the truth and asked Ben to teach my grandpa how to garden. Francisco learned that it is better to tell the truth than to lie.

Rosa's writing is clearer and more organized. She displayed knowledge of the events in the book through her mentioning that the flowers were ruined. She referred to ideas not clearly stated by the author. Some of these thoughts include that grandpa probably couldn't garden because he was from Mexico City and that Ben would have to find someone else to replant the flowers. She also demonstrated an understanding of the difference between cause and effect when she indicated that the flowers would not have been destroyed and grandpa would not have been so embarrassed if Francisco had never lied.

 # Fitting Instruction to Meet the Needs of the Student
Making the Goal of Instruction Meaningful to Rosa and the Students

Rosa and the other students did not view reading as something that they did to gain meaning and enjoyment. Rosa didn't stop herself when the text didn't make sense or to think about the ideas in the text. It also took a while for her to see that she could make a difference in her reading by engaging in the strategies we talked about in class. I found it necessary to get them to move through the motions of facilitator, before they knew how to make the strategies their own. I saw a big change in Rosa and the students as they moved from reading words on a page as a "school required" activity to engaging in meaningful ideas about the texts they read.

Instructional Methods That Helped Rosa Engage in RT Strategies

It took a lot of modeling to help Rosa and the other students understand how to facilitate the strategies and discussion. I also realized that they were so dependent on me that I had to provide role cards to help them use the strategies. At first they performed these roles systematically, but at least began to think and engage in predicting, clarifying, questioning, and summarizing. Later they were less dependent on the role prompts and used the strategies when they made sense to develop their meaning making of the texts. I was just beginning to see Rosa apply these strategies in her independent reading. She did better when engaging in talk with others. We were able to accomplish this somewhat in our teacher-student conferences. It made me learn about how important it is to give students the opportunities to engage in talk about books with others, and not to just answer questions to assess their comprehension or write responses without talking about books with others. Their RT discussions began to reflect what we do as lifelong readers.

Instructional Materials That Promoted Greater Engagement

In taking a careful look at Rosa's progress with reciprocal teaching, I noticed that she was more engaged with some texts than others. These included texts that the students could relate to because of their background or the kinds of similar problems that characters faced in the stories. I became more aware of choosing culturally relevant texts for them and providing more introduction and background when texts focused on topics that were unfamiliar. For example, reading a text about a surveyor of a village where people use the woods to travel introduces some very unfamiliar topics for many of the city-raised students in my room.

Rosa, along with the other members of the group, improved greatly. The students had begun truly thinking about what they were reading. They also began enjoying reading and talking with each other. Because of Rosa's perseverance and success during the year, she was awarded "Most Improved" at graduation.

References

Beaver, J. (1997). *Developmental reading assessment*. Parsippany, NJ: Celebration.

Brock, B. (1982). *No flying in the house*. New York: Harper Collins Children's Books.

Bunting, E. (2004). *A day's work*. New York: Houghton Mifflin.

Cleary, B. (1990). *Henry Huggins* [50th anniversary edition]. New York: Harper Collins.

Duke, N. K., & Pearson, P. (2002). Effective practices for developing reading comprehension. In A. E. Farstrup & S. Samuels (Eds.), *What research has to say about reading instruction* (pp. 205–242). Newark, DE: International Reading Association.

Fountas, I. C., & Pinnell, G. S. (2001). *Guiding Readers and Writers Grades 3–6*. Portsmouth, NH: Heinemann.

Havill, J. (1989). *Jamaica tag along*. New York: Houghton Mifflin.

King, C. M., & Parent Johnson, L. M. (1999). Constructing meaning via reciprocal teaching. *Reading Research & Instruction, 38*(3), 169–186.

LaFleur, B. (Jan/Feb 2005). Forgotten cowboys. *National Geographic Explorer, 4*, 18–21.

Martel, C. (1995). *Yagua days*. New York: Houghton Mifflin.

McLaughlin, M., & Allen, M. B. (2002). *Guided comprehension: A teaching model for grades 3–8*. Newark, DE: International Reading Association.

New Zealand Ministry of Education (1993). *Reciprocal teaching: Extending reading strategies* [video].

Oczkus, L. D. (2003). *Reciprocal teaching at work*. Newark, DE: International Reading Association.

Palincsar, A. S., & Brown, A. L. (1984). Reciprocal teaching of comprehension-fostering and comprehension-monitoring activities. *Cognition & Instruction 1*(2), 117–175.

The Reading and Writing Project Teachers College (2004, February) 6–9 Quick Reading Assessment, Columbia University.

Williams, V. B. (1984). *A chair for my mother*. New York: Harper Collins.

7 | Engaging in Book Talks

Supporting a Fifth Grader to Build on the
Ideas of Others

Margaret Falcone, Tutor and Education Graduate Student

"People read because they might have to do a book report."
Fifth Grader, Nikki

Nikki was referred to me for tutoring because of her parents' concerns about her lack of interest in reading independently. During our first tutoring session, as a way of getting to know Nikki as a student, I asked her if she wanted to share any of her schoolwork with me. She excitedly showed me her school journals and personal song book. Nikki was proud of her work and had many good ideas:

My toes are priceless their one of a kind. When I am angrey they trot like a mule. When I am joyful the prance like a ballarina. My toes huddle together like a daddy penguin holding his egg, when I am worried. My feelings are represented by my toes.

Nikki was a thoughtful writer, who had been touched by the poetry of the late Mattie J. T. Stepanek. Nikki especially loved his poem titled "Heartsong" (Stepanek, 2002). Mattie's writing spoke to her in a way that Nikki could understand and relate to. She "sort of" (Nikki's favorite term) shared the same feeling as Mattie, that you can experience happiness in simply listening to your heart. Nikki's writing reflected her innocence and acceptance of herself and the world around her. When Nikki wrote, she used invented spellings. Nikki was aware that her approximations needed to be replaced with conventional spelling. When I told her, "Let me know how I can help you," Nikki responded, "I need some help in spelling and writing."

Nikki, however, didn't share the same enthusiasm about reading. I needed to inquire more to learn about her as a reader. In a reading interview, I asked Nikki, "What have you learned from reading?" Her response was, "There are a lot of words that you don't know in some books and reading helps you try to figure out the words." As I listened to Nikki's response, I noticed what she didn't say. For Nikki, reading was often about getting through the words than the meaning between and beyond those words.

The First Hurdle: Nikki as an Engaged Reader

Nikki came to me as a fifth-grade student whose teacher informed her that she needed to do more independent reading. Independent reading is a mandatory task for students in area public schools in order to meet an educational promotional standard. When asked in a reading interview, "How do you feel about the reading that you do at home?" Nikki responded, "When you read separately, I am not really into it." When I inquired, "How do you decide what to read about?" Nikki responded, "Usually my teacher assigns it for me."

In one of our after-school tutoring sessions, Nikki and I shared in the reading of a self-selected, easy book. She admitted choosing it as a quick read to fulfill her teacher's expectations for an independent book report that was due to be handed in that day. Together, we judged the book to be "too easy" with respect to vocabulary, and we determined it a text appropriate for a beginning reader. Collaborating in this way together made Nikki's views on reading visible to me. She did not expect to come away from her reading experience with anything more than the credit earned for having read a book. I believed that my role would be to help Nikki choose narrative texts appropriate to her level and interest, and to engage her in meaningful talk about books.

Knowing Where to Begin

Getting to know how Nikki sees herself as a reader and writer helped me to think about her uniqueness, and what she brought to our sessions in terms of her experiences and attitudes. I gathered information from a variety of assessment measures to determine Nikki's needs as I aimed to help her become an engaged reader. These included:

- Qualitative Reading Inventory-4 (QRI-4) (Leslie & Caldwell, 2006)
- Nikki's report cards and parent-teacher conference
- Informal Reading Interview (Fountas & Pinnell, 2002)

Qualitative Reading Inventory-4

In the first week of our tutoring sessions, I assessed Nikki's independent reading ability using narrative passages from the QRI-4 (Leslie & Caldwell, 2006). My assessments indicated that she was able to comprehend fourth-grade level texts. Nikki was able to retell a narrative passage with a fair amount of accuracy. Nikki's responses to explicit comprehension questions on this Level 4 narrative were more informed than those she made to implied questions. Nikki's challenge with implicit questions and thinking beyond a literal interpretation of a text was also confirmed when talking with her classroom teacher.

Report Cards and Parent-Teacher Conference

Nikki progressed toward meeting grade-level standards in her classroom work and learning behaviors as indicated on her fourth-grade year-end and fifth-grade first-quarter report cards. Nikki's fourth- and fifth-grade teachers' written comments indicated that she needed more confidence in herself and to participate more. Her fourth-grade classroom teacher reported her overall performance on reading, writing, and listening and speaking standards to be satisfactory for her grade-level. However, within the standard of listening and speaking, Nikki's performance only approached standards in "builds on the ideas of others in conversation." Nikki's first-quarter report card in fifth grade also reflected the same performance level in this area. This standard considers students' expressive language skills and ability to make one's thinking visible to others during discussions (Board of Education of the City of New York, 1997).

Nikki's parents and I met with her fifth-grade teacher for the fall parent-teacher conference. Her teacher explained to us that Nikki was an attentive listener during her whole-group lessons. She shared with us that Nikki had a constant willingness to offer her help to classmates who were challenged with new material or projects and worked with them cooperatively. However, she had observed that Nikki lacked self-confidence in the area of classroom participation. Nikki rarely raised her hand during a language arts lesson; she voluntarily raised her hand only when she was certain that her answer was correct.

Nikki's teacher administered a reading test in the beginning of the school year that assessed students' knowledge and use of their specific reading strategies when they read. Nikki's answers showed that she needed to work on strengthening her comprehension skills in understanding plot and analyzing character. Her teacher also asked me to work on Nikki's inferential thinking skills. In addition, her teacher shared that on her fourth-grade NYS English Language Arts exam, Nikki scored only 71% for critical analysis.

Reading Interview

I interviewed Nikki orally with a reading interview (Fountas & Pinnell, 2001) to find out information about her as a reader. I asked Nikki questions about her reading interests and independent reading point of view. Nikki's responses showed that she wasn't hooked on reading:

MARGARET: Why do people read?

NIKKI: Because they might have to do a book report. Maybe they want to.

MARGARET: What have you learned from reading?

NIKKI: There are a lot of words that you don't know in some books and reading helps you try to figure out the word.

> **MARGARET:**   What would you like to learn how to do better as a reader?
>
> **NIKKI:**   I would like to learn how to read faster without skimming.

Nikki didn't like to read. She didn't identify herself as a player in this game called reading, but instead saw herself as a bystander. Nikki needed to be invited to participate, not simply watch the game being played.

 ## Literacy Challenges: Learner and Teacher

Nikki needed someone to show her that reading had benefits beyond having to do a book report or to fill time when she was bored. She did not entertain the thought that reading could be anything other than learning new words and their meanings. I needed to find a way to convince her that her personal involvement was an essential starting point in establishing new reading behaviors and extending her thinking about literary texts.

Looking for a Discussion Approach to Initiate Nikki's Involvement

My initial impression of book discussions was that our conversation would flow naturally. I came to our sessions with an agenda, having read the assigned reading material and prepared to cover certain points and topics, which I thought were important and interesting. I asked Nikki inferential questions about key plot events, character motivations, and my perception of the author's message. However, I often found myself alone in these discussions and answering my own questions, because I couldn't seem to draw her in. Consequently, I reverted to asking recall-type questions to encourage Nikki to make her voice heard. When Nikki did respond to my inquisitions, it was with short and concise one-word answers, such as yes-no replies or "I don't know." Her voice was often represented by inaudible utterances such as "hmm" as evidenced in our book talk on Jerry Spinelli's *Stargirl*, a book recommended to Nikki by her teacher. In this book, readers meet a free-spirited and caring teenage girl who did not fit in with her peers. Stargirl falls for a boy, who returns her feelings, but who finds that being connected with her forces him to grapple with the harshness of mainstream teen culture, to which he belongs.

> **MARGARET:**   Leo keeps on trying to stay away. Now, where's Leo?
>
> **NIKKI:**   Hmm, in the driveway.
>
> **MARGARET:**   Yes, what did Stargirl do?
>
> **NIKKI:**   Put Cinnamon down.

MARGARET: Okay, but what did she actually do? Stargirl must have caught sight of him from her window. So what did she do?

NIKKI: Go outside and asked him questions.

MARGARET: Yes, she went right up to him.

NIKKI: Hmm, hmm.

MARGARET: Do you think he is afraid to be noticed? Or did he actually take that first step and he let her help him. What do you think?

NIKKI: He took the first step.

MARGARET: He took a step and what did she do?

NIKKI: Help him.

MARGARET: Help him. Could you say that Stargirl is sort of like a helper?

NIKKI: Hmm.

Nikki met my approach to interaction with indifference, and it became clear that our discussions were not based on a give-and-take, but on me leading and Nikki listening and responding. I was challenged by Nikki's seeming indifference to our discussions, and my own feelings of failure to motivate her engagement in reading. It seemed so natural for Nikki to listen and to follow along that I began to audiotape our sessions to get a better understanding of my teaching, and why we were not engaging in true literary discussions.

After weeks of sessions in which I saw no progression in Nikki's involvement in our discussions and which increased my frustration with the inquisition style of interacting with literature, I realized that I needed to explore other strategy options aimed at helping her to build on the ideas of others. I looked to the literature on book discussions and comprehension. In my search, I came across information on two approaches to reading comprehension: Question-Answer Relationships (QAR) (Raphael & Au, 2005; Raphael & Pearson, 1985) and a graphic organizer based on Bloom's Taxonomy called the Skyscraper (Paziotopoulos & Kroll, 2004).

QARs enhances readers' knowledge to the importance of context and information sources to participate in book discussions. The QAR framework offers readers a common vocabulary to think about questions and where one might find the answers as "In the Book" or "In My Head." I attempted to implement this approach in my sessions with Nikki. I felt awkward using the QAR vocabulary, such as "Right There," "Think & Search," and "Author & Me," with a fifth-grade student as we interacted and discussed text. Nikki knew the mechanics of how to identify information sources and what a question asked. What Nikki was unfamiliar with was how to extend her thinking and initiate a personal response to literature. Using QAR as an approach to build on her ideas was not a good fit for my purpose of initiating involvement because it helped perpetuate our inquisition style of interacting. After listening to the tape of our 12th session, I wrote in my teaching journal:

> I need to find a purpose for our questioning. We need a concrete direction. I find a need to modify the QAR approach in order to gradually transfer the discussion from teacher-led to student-centered. (Teaching Journal, Session 12)

I knew that I wanted to cultivate a new type of interactive relationship among Nikki, the text, and myself where power was distributed and our collective efforts constructed new meanings. The process of QAR did not suit our needs for a true discussion; therefore, my search continued.

The Skyscraper (Paziotopoulos & Kroll, 2004) is a planning tool that two teachers created by adapting the six levels of Bloom's taxonomy for use as a guide to help students learn to expand their view of thinking of narrative or expository text. The Skyscraper is an authentic model that helps learners imagine moving up the stairs of a tall building to achieve higher levels of information processing, using prompts relevant to each level: get the facts (Knowledge) → understand the facts (Comprehension) → make a connection to real life (Application) → look for patterns while gathering information (Analysis) → expand on information to make predictions (Synthesis) → expression of personal opinions on the topic (Evaluation) (Paziotopoulos & Kroll, 2004, pp. 673–674). I implemented this planning tool as a way to guide my line of questioning to initiate Nikki into our discussions. The following excerpt is from our book talk on the chapter "Lost" from Sharon Creech's *Granny Torrelli Makes Soup* (2005). This book is about a grandmother who gives advice to her 12-year-old granddaughter, as they make soup together, about what to do when you are angry with someone you love. The book leads readers through the granddaughter's process of remembering the good things about her best friend; the nice things he had said and done for her; and why she liked him in the first place.

MARGARET: Who was lost? (Knowledge Question)

NIKKI: Hmm, Bailey was.

MARGARET: Bailey was lost. Summarize to me—how did he get lost? (Comprehension Question)

NIKKI: Hmm, it was supposed to be a short walk, but it became a long walk for him because he is blind.

MARGARET: Okay, excellent response. Why do you think Bailey got upset when Rosie said that he was lost? (Analysis Question)

NIKKI: Because he didn't really think that he was lost, it was just because he was blind and he didn't know what happened because he was blind and he couldn't see, but it was really supposed to be a short walk.

After this session, I reflected in my journal:

> I feel my questions using the Skyscraper as a planning guide prompted Nikki to give more expanded responses, besides Yes or No and I don't know. However, Nikki did not demonstrate the ability to build on my questioning. After she responded, she appeared finished with the question and did not expand upon the dialogue. Questioning became rote and mechanical for the both of us. Based on my observations on our discussion today, the planning guide did not support a relationship among myself, the text and Nikki. She answered my questions as if she was taking a standardized test. Each question Nikki answered seemed not to build upon the next; rather she treated it as if it was distinct from one another. (Teacher Journal, Session 13)

As the leader of our discussions, I assumed it was my responsibility to make Nikki aware of how the author was working through the literary elements in helping her make sense of the text. I worked diligently to elicit responses from Nikki, in hindsight maybe too hard. An experienced teacher once commented that you should never work harder than your student; both of you need to share in the responsibility of a discussion.

> In hindsight, after listening to myself on tape and digging into the research literature on discussions, I am coming to dislike questioning. The notion of questioning becomes automatized and turns on an inquisition button in me when my questions have been correctly answered. Asking questions that are important to each of us will differ because of our age, experience and intent (to name a few), and has the potential not to meet people where they are at—we each had our own agenda. In order to have a true discussion, there must be a connection, a mutual interest and purpose in mind. (Teacher Journal, Postscript, Session 13)

I continued to ponder what type of context I could give Nikki where I could move away from inquisitions and be responsive to her unique interpretation of the text. I wanted to move from central authority figure to facilitator (Almasi, 1995) or co-participant.

Building on Nikki's Ideas in Conversations

In order for Nikki to build on the ideas of others in conversation, she needed to gain experience in being able to initiate involvement. I was talking too much, controlling the direction of the conversation, and not encouraging Nikki to build on her own ideas. When Nikki tried to initiate involvement, her responses fell on deaf ears. She did try to initiate involvement in our conversations, as seen in the following excerpt from Sharon Creech's *Granny Torrelli Makes Soup*:

NIKKI: Granny Torrelli, hmm, felt left out. Did you ever feel left out?

MARGARET: Did I ever feel left out? Well, how did Granny feel left out with Pardo?

I was unaccustomed to this new behavior from Nikki, and I did not know how to respond effectively. This prevented me from building on her thinking. I was a learner who needed to hone my self-control skills to listen more and give her opportunity to take the conversation in her direction. My planned agenda prompted me to resort to asking questions and subsequently disengaged her from our discussions. Nikki's hurdle in recognizing and building on the thoughts of others applied to me, too, as a beginning teacher. I needed to learn how to value her thoughts and listen more effectively.

 ## Addressing the Challenges

If Nikki could motivate and engage herself in the process of drawing on her life experiences to form emotional responses in writing poetry, then perhaps her literacy challenges lay in thinking about and responding to ideas and experiences from different points of view. How could I address these challenges and move both of us forward and proceed with a true discussion?

Implementing a Framework for Discussion (Seed and Three Thoughts)

I was in search of a discussion, a framework for talk, which would give Nikki autonomy to search within text or her own knowledge for advancing our discussions, rather than depending on me to sustain our conversations, as seen in the following excerpt of our conversations on Sharon Creech's *Granny Torrelli Makes Soup*:

> MARGARET: On page 3, I have a question. Has anyone said to you "get over yourself"?
>
> NIKKI: No.
>
> MARGARET: What do you think Bailey meant when he said "get over yourself" to Rosie?
>
> NIKKI: Hmm, they need to stop thinking of themselves and to think of other people, too.
>
> MARGARET: Okay, let's keep that in mind for when we keep reading because that might be the key to why Bailey is so upset with Rosie and why she hates him. Do you really think from reading up to page 34 that Rosie hates Bailey?
>
> NIKKI: No.
>
> MARGARET: Enough to end the friendship?
>
> NIKKI: No.

MARGARET: Okay. Now Granny Torrelli comes over to Rosie's house and they start to make soup. Granny Torrelli also makes Rosie laugh. Has anyone made you laugh when you felt sad?

NIKKI: Ahmm.

Villaume, Worden, Williams, Hopkins, and Rosenblatt (1994) were five educators who were in search of a discussion. Their collective experiences in the classroom inspired them to introduce to their students a framework for discussion that supported reading and talking about narrative texts from an aesthetic stance, where emphasis was on the readers' engagement. I hit the jackpot! I finally found an approach that was a good fit for Nikki and me. The discussion seed was an approach to reading with which Nikki could identify with as a writer, because she had acquired prior knowledge of seed writing in her fifth-grade classroom. In several of our sessions, Nikki shared with me essays she had written for homework using the seed format. The approach allowed her ideas to shine through while letting her remain focused on the task at hand. This framework for discussion required collaborating partners to write a discussion seed, defined as one important idea about the book being read, and three thoughts about that seed.

Nikki was introduced to the concept of the discussion seed in our 15th session, along with instructions on seed writing that incorporated seed prompts or phrases for beginning her seed starters. The starters recommended for her seed writing were: "I wonder . . ." and "I really felt a part of the book when. . . ." Based on my reading about discussion seeds, effective seeds grew to more meaningful or expanded discussions. These seeds are open-ended ideas that reflect information such as readers' inferential explanations of plot events or their interpretations of characters' feelings and ideas. Less effective seeds are difficult for students to talk and elaborate on. These seeds are closed-ended ideas where students did not expand on information in the book, but instead made easily identifiable predictions not based on synthesis of the material; related general (rather than specific) connections to the book; or explained favorite facts.

This concept of a discussion seed had potential to address Nikki's literacy challenge of building on her ideas in conversation and expanding on her thinking (literal to conceptual) about text. Below are Nikki's first seed starters for Kate DiCamillo's *Because of Winn Dixie* (2001). This book is about a lonely, motherless preacher's daughter who moved in the summer of her 10th year to a town in Florida. Readers get to meet a young girl who is on her own a lot, good with words, and determined to fill the void in her heart that is caused by missing her mother.

Nikki used the language of the discussion seed and related thoughts that I had introduced to her. Although her responses were not producing grand

I wonder if India Opal will make friends.

1. I didn't think she will because she lives in an adult-only trailer park.
2. She might make a friend at the Winn-Dixie food mart.
3. I think she might make another friend that is a stray dog.

I really felt a part of the book when she said she felt like an orphan because she really has no one except Winn-Dixie.

1. Her dad is too busy with preaching or doing things with preaching.
2. Her mom left.

Nikki's seed starters for *Because of Winn Dixie* (DiCamillo, 2001).

conversations, Nikki's responses freed her from the constraints of my inquisitions that had driven our discussions. Instead the seeds offered Nikki the motivation to gradually assume responsibility to depend on her own cognitive resources, abilities, and feelings to determine what the text meant to her.

Learning to Be Responsive to Ideas

It wasn't until I read about grand conversations (see Eeds & Wells, 1989) that I realized that my inexperience as a beginning teacher was prompting me to romanticize about an ideal book discussion. I did not take my cues from Nikki: what she was interested in and what had piqued her interest. When I reflected about our participatory roles during our sessions, I realized that Nikki's inexperience in initiating and elaborating on her ideas of text was due in part to my lack of experience in knowing how to provide supportive, empowering, and meaningful contexts. I was not versed in the art of grand conversations. What was preventing me from being responsive?

I shared my frustration on my inability to engage Nikki in our discussions with an experienced teacher. In this meeting, I shared Nikki's most recent seed response for *Because of Winn Dixie*, which had disappointed me because she wrote about the minor characters in the story and not any of the ideas I saw as key to the chapters.

I wonder why the bald headed boys called the lady a witchHe seems nice.

1. Did the boys ever meet her.
2. Bubba likes peanut butter.

Nikki's seed starters for *Because of Winn Dixie* (DiCamillo, 1991).

My experienced colleague made a thoughtful observation about Nikki's ideas and my challenges in engaging Nikki in meaningful discussions. I had seen Nikki as responding to insignificant details in the story. My colleague reminded me that authors choose minor characters very deliberately to interact with the main characters and develop important plots. It seemed to her that I unwittingly prejudged Nikki's ideas when they differed from my own. Nikki was writing about her ideas and thoughts in ways that made her extended thinking visible.

I was surprised by what I heard, and yet I was preempted from being responsive to Nikki's collaborating effort. I knew I had missed an opportunity to say, "That is a good idea, I never thought of it that way," or "That's interesting, tell me more." Nikki's seed ideas on *Because of Winn Dixie* addressed the author's portrayal of theme and showed her initiative to think deeply about the text, without deliberate intent. Nikki was making observations and drawing conclusions about minor characters' feelings and behaviors that helped her to comprehend the main character in response to plot events. By not responding to Nikki's ideas, I was depriving her of the opportunity to extend her thinking about her interpretation of characters' motivations, and I was not helping her to identify the author's message. I did not empower Nikki with the knowledge that everything has a purpose, no matter how minor or major. Most important, I was now learning from these very insightful ideas. Prejudging Nikki's response contributed to our breakdown in communication that session and did not empower her to engage in working collaboratively with me. I needed to meet Nikki where her experiences, interests, and ideas about literature were evident, and then help extend these ideas to achieve deeper textual understanding.

After much reflection, my next move seemed obvious. I chose to initiate Nikki into our discussions by inviting her to begin the session.

> **MARGARET:**   I am going to leave it up to you where to begin. Do you want to go through your seed starters first, or do you want to tell me how you felt about these three chapters in *Because of Winn Dixie*?
>
> **NIKKI:**   Hmm, seed starters.
>
> **MARGARET:**   Fine, go ahead.
>
> **NIKKI:**   My, hmm, my first seed starter was: I felt a part of the book when Opal asks Miss Franny to take home some of the candy. Hmm, my first thought: it was nice that Opal was thinking of people.
>
> **MARGARET:**   Okay, let's talk about that. You thought it was nice that Opal was thinking of people.
>
> **NIKKI:**   Ahmm.
>
> **MARGARET:**   What made you write that?

NIKKI: Because in this book, if she sees something that she likes, she might take it home. But it seems like that she doesn't really share, because it's not like she's selfish. She doesn't share because she might not have anything, but she might have no one to share it with. Like, so she doesn't really ask for things to take home.

MARGARET: What made you think of that thought?

NIKKI: Hmm, because she started caring. She cares about Otis, well sort of like this because she is thinking of Otis. She is thinking of other people, too.

Given the opportunity to initiate discussion and for me to sit back and encourage her to take time to explain her thoughts, Nikki made some very insightful comments. Nikki was genuinely empathizing with the characters, not merely reading the words and getting through the texts. Most important, as I listened, I, too, saw the book in a new way.

Strengthening Nikki's Critical Thinking Skills

Readers are invited to engage themselves in the information read in a text, and depending on the purposes set for the reading and the teacher's approach to social interaction, the connections they make are the ones that their experience has enabled them to make. Nikki needed a frame of reference for how she should exerience a narrative when reading independently and discussing collaboratively with me. She needed to be informed about our purpose for reading literature (Rosenblatt, 1991). Adopting an aesthetic stance toward the text engaged Nikki in what the words alluded to, what she was experiencing, thinking, and feeling during her reading. My former inquisitions had promoted conflicts with text. They gave Nikki information about the gist of the story, but did not spur her to become involved in a relationship with text and to move forward and initiate an extended response to literature. Soon, we were having conversations where both of us were sharing and responding to each other.

NIKKI: When I wrote my seed, I was surprised that Gloria drank, because I was sort of like Opal she was surprised that she did that many bad things. I was surprised that she drank because I wouldn't expect her to drink.

MARGARET: Sometimes people are not who you think they are, but that does not mean that makes them bad or good, they are just different from you. Sometimes we can't rely on our expectations. It's the reality of who people are and that is how you judge them for yourself, whether you want to be a friend with them or not. It's not what you expect them to be, it's who they are. What did you think about what I had to say about why we read this chapter out loud?

NIKKI: I think it was so important because everything that people say is important and that it's sort of because this teaches a lesson, sort of like Granny Torrelli because this Opal would be Rosie and Granny Torrelli would be Mrs. Dump because Granny Torrelli and Gloria Dump are always giving advice. That I think that it was important because, it actually just hit me now. . . .

MARGARET: What?

NIKKI: Because I . . . no, because I was thinking about what I had to say about what she said, and I thought it was important. The chapter really taught us a lesson into starting conversations better, because we really weren't doing it. And it sort of was important because we re-read an important lesson not to judge someone for what they were but how they are now.

MARGARET: And you make a good point.

"We may worry less about transmitting, measuring and judging and more about cultivating students' growth and development, their gradual creating of their own conceptual world" (Probst, 1986, p. 60). When I focused on offering Nikki an opportunity to shape her experiences and develop a personal voice based on her own ideas about text, I gave her an invitation to literature.

 ## Fitting Instruction to Meet the Needs of the Reader

My actions during the early days of our book talk did not reflect my agenda: to initiate Nikki's involvement in discussions and to help her build on the ideas of others. Instead, I used an inquisition style of interaction, and my teacher-initiated topics pushed Nikki further away from leading the discussions at any point. All too often teachers like me don't really listen to others. We concentrate so hard on what we are doing that we never really hear what others are saying. The message we are sending is, "I don't care what you think. But *you* should listen to *me*."

From Inquisitions to Collaborative Interactions

When readers search for meaning, they are approaching literature with a specific purpose in mind. Rosenblatt and other educators support the notion that the meaning in literature is neither in the reader nor on the written page alone, but part of the transaction between reader, text, and other readers. Consequently, teachers are not viewed as authorities on meaning but simply other readers to talk with (Probst, 1986). Reading without a purpose is not transacting with the text, but simply going through the motions of fulfilling the teacher's expectations for the discussion. In listening back to our conversations, I realized that I tried engaging Nikki in our discussions of literature in a procedural way, where I maintained control of the interaction and asked questions on issues that were important to me (Almasi, 1995). When Nikki's responses differed from my own, I tried to impress my point of view on her. I did not respect and validate her opinion, nor did I engage her with a follow-up response. The following is an excerpt from one of our earlier taped sessions on Sharon Creech's *Love That Dog*. This book is about an elementary school-age boy who learns how to express his feelings about his life experiences writing poetry with the help and support of his teacher. Although I chose the book because of Nikki's love for poetry, I didn't give her a chance to share her own ideas about the book.

> MARGARET: Let's think about what Miss Stretchberry did for Jack. Nikki, what did she do for Jack?
>
> NIKKI: Every time he couldn't write or he didn't want to write, hmm, Miss Stretchberry read a poem that helped him and then he was able to write poetry.
>
> MARGARET: Okay. But the reason why he couldn't write poetry was because he didn't want to? He had no ideas or because he was afraid to?
>
> NIKKI: He didn't want to.
>
> MARGARET: Okay, I disagree. I think he was afraid to for two reasons. One being when something is new, sometimes people are afraid to do something. And I think the second reason for me, at least, would be because in this poem, 'Tears,' we know from reading the book now, that Jack had tears of loss for his dog. . . . What did Miss Stretchberry do? She gave Jack kindness, her trust and respect by giving him the class poems to help bring out his voice so that he could write about his dog. And by writing, do you think that it helped him and gave him comfort? What do you think?
>
> NIKKI: Yes.
>
> MARGARET: Well let's elaborate on that.

Developing engagement in literature is an invitation to search in text and self for the sources of meaning that makes up the uniqueness of the reader (Probst, 1986). It is not a step-by-step technique that can be transmitted from one person to another. Engagement is a meaning-making experience that requires readers to integrate information once it is located to formulate a personal response based on their motivation, personal involvement, and use of higher-level thinking skills.

Nikki's personal involvement and willingness to elaborate on her relationships with literature was made possible by my implementation of the framework of a discussion seed and three thoughts and a conscious effort to support social interaction and to listen to her ideas. This framework helped to extend

Nikki's thinking to construct a personal response to literary elements. As I encouraged Nikki to share her ideas and listened without judging, Nikki gained the confidence to share her interpretations as I moved my emphasis to sharing ideas, rather than her correctness. The following excerpt of our taped conversation of Kate DiCamillo's *Because of Winn Dixie* shows Nikki acting and talking like a reader:

MARGARET: Tell us about your second thought.

NIKKI: I think that Gloria gave Opal something to think about, and Gloria opened Opal's eyes.

MARGARET: What did she give Opal to think about?

NIKKI: Like how it's nice when you have a second chance sort of because Gloria Dump hasn't been in jail but she has done a lot of bad things because of a lot of whiskey and beer and wine, sort of like of Georgie's mom and Opal's mom. She stops drinking whiskey, and sort of has a fresh start.

MARGARET: What did she give Opal to think about? What did she say to her?

NIKKI: Anyone can do something bad sometimes.

MARGARET: And what does Gloria say to Opal: You've got to remember, you can't always judge people by the things they have done in the past. You've got to judge them by what they are doing now.

NIKKI: Gloria opened Opal's eyes from that because now she like sort of knows that people might have done a bad thing but now they might be good.

Writing her discussion seeds and related thoughts was an effective tool for Nikki because she saw herself as a writer, and her engagement in her seed thoughts gave our discussions meaning. As our discussions began to be centered on the notion of the discussion seed and three thoughts, I observed Nikki's engagement in reading and in the extension of her thinking as she began to initiate, facilitate, and respond to my supportive and responsive style of participatory talk.

References

Almasi, J. F. (1995). The nature of fourth graders' sociocognitive conflicts in peer-led and teacher-led discussions of literature. *Reading Research Quarterly, 30*(3), 314–351.

Board of Education of the City of New York (1997). *New standards in performance standards for English language arts*. New York: Board of Education of the City of New York.

Creech, S. (2003). *Love that dog*. New York: Harper Collins.

Creech, S. (2005). *Granny Torelli makes soup*. New York: Harper Collins.

DiCamillo, K. (2001). *Because of Winn Dixie*. Cambridge, MA: Candlewick.

Eeds, M., & Wells, D. (1989). Grand conversations: An exploration of meaning construction in literature study groups. *Research in the Teaching of English, 23*(1), 4–29.

Fountas, I. C., & Pinnell, G. S. (2001). *Guiding readers and writers grades 3–6: Teaching comprehension, genre, and content literacy*. Portsmouth, NH: Heinemann.

Leslie, L., & Caldwell, J. (2006). *Qualitative reading inventory—4*. New York: Pearson Education.

Paziotopoulos, A., & Kroll, M. (2004). Hooked on thinking. *The Reading Teacher, 57*, 672–677.

Probst, R. E. (1986). Three relationships in the teaching of literature. *English Journal, 75*, 60–68.

Raphael, T. E., & Au, R. (2005). QAR: Enhancing comprehension and test taking across grades and content areas. *The Reading Teacher, 59*(3), 206–221.

Raphael, T. E., & Pearson, P. D. (1985). Increasing students' awareness of sources of information for answering questions. *American Educational Research Journal, 22*, 217–235.

Rosenblatt, L. M. (1991). LITERATURE—S.O.S.! *Language Arts, 68*, 444–448.

Spinelli, J. (2004). *Stargirl*. New York: Random House Children's Books.

Stepanek, M. J. T. (2002). *Heartsongs*. New York: Hyperion.

Villaume, S. K., Worden, S. W., Williams, S., Hopkins, L., & Rosenblatt, C. (1994). Five teachers in search of a discussion. *The Reading Teacher, 47*(6), 480–487.

8 | Creating a Culturally Relevant Learning Community

Inviting a Sixth Grader to Read and Discuss Texts

Arin Marcus Rusch, Sixth-Grade Teacher

"I hate to read!"
Sixth Grader, Juan

Juan was one of my sixth-grade students who actively resisted school. In morning periods, he often put his head on his desk as if he hadn't slept the night before. At other times Juan would have outbursts, expressing how much he hated school or teachers. During lessons he'd spend more time trying to socialize with his peers than participating in the learning activity. On several occasions I confronted his disruptive behavior, both in class and privately, and in either situation his response was, "It's not fair." After I met with his mother, he expressed anger that I had talked with her and did not show any improvement. Juan was one of many students in my school who came to school, but didn't see a purpose in it for him.

Juan as a Reader and Writer

Juan avoided reading, often by spending our reading time "getting ready" to read, without ever turning a page or responding in his journal. He started several books and put them down. I had not yet seen him finish a book. He rarely participated in discussions about literature, and when he raised his hand to speak, he often decided not to say what he was planning, and instead said, "Forget it," as if he had lost confidence in his idea. His writing behaviors were similar, often never getting past the heading on his paper or a first sentence. He did, however, participate in discussion when he could refer back to his own experiences. My assessments revealed that he had the ability to read at a fourth-grade level, based on informal reading assessments and his citywide test scores from the previous spring.

The First Hurdle: Giving Juan a Reason to Read

When asked to complete the sentence "Reading is . . ." a standard response from students in my sixth grade class was "boring." Some students were not so mild and inserted words such as "stupid" or "awful." Juan was quick to tell you how much he hated to read. Although Juan's response was discouraging and in sharp contrast to my own reading experiences, it didn't surprise me. Juan struggled with reading and lacked many of the reading skills he needed. Furthermore, and perhaps because of his limited skills, enthusiasm for reading in my classroom seemed woefully low, at best.

Motivation and comprehension are linked together in a mutual relationship. Students experience more reading success if they are interested, and likewise students are more interested if they are successful. It is widely accepted that literacy motivation plays a critical role in literacy learning and achievement. An important first step toward comprehension is the motivation to read (Gambrell, 1996). My experiences have shown that if motivation is not present, it is difficult to provide students like Juan with meaningful tools for comprehension. However, with tools for comprehension and with a reading purpose, a student can be an engaged reader. With that greater ability to comprehend, the student can begin to develop an intrinsic motivation to learn and continue reading (Jordan & Hendricks, 2002). Thus, for reading success, both motivation and comprehension tools must be present.

Although they rely heavily on each other, motivation and comprehension are also linked by a common theme: both depend on the reader's ability to connect to the text. This seems obviously necessary in motivation—"getting into" a book is making a connection, personal or otherwise, to that text (Kong & Fitch, 2002). Recognizing the importance of the student-to-text connection, in which kids are able to identify themselves in some way through the text, it seemed clear to me that this was not happening for Juan or most of my students. The more I thought about the texts my students had access to, the more it seemed that any connection would be remote. The classroom library was filled with outdated books, often falling apart, with outdated covers depicting scenes that starkly contrasted with my students' realities. Few books took place in cities. Few dealt with settings, families, and social issues that remotely resembled those my students lived with. Overall, the lack of culturally relevant texts was obvious.

Not only are most of the texts that students try to read in school irrelevant to their lives, students like Juan often don't seem to see themselves as part of an academic, literate community at all. Because of this disconnect between school and their own lives, students have little encouragement to develop and assert their *own* identity as learners and readers. I realized that none of the everyday texts that Juan and my students see and use outside of school was making its way into classroom use. I (and I suspect teachers before me) had been teaching reading, for the most part, as an action isolated from my students. Because of this, for Juan, reading in school was a required chore, unconnected to anything that is actually relevant to his life, family, or future. My challenge then was to consider Juan's experiences and interests to give him a reason to read while in school.

 ## Knowing Where to Begin

I decided that I would make a concerted effort to create a more culturally relevant learning community in my classroom. To determine what changes I wanted to make, I reflected on my practice, consulted the literature, and most importantly listened to my students. My sources included:

- Research on my students' community
- Professional literature on culturally relevant teaching
- Student surveys
- Student reading assessments

My Students' Community

The middle school (grades 6–8) where I teach is in an urban, low-income neighborhood. According to the current U.S. Census, more than one-quarter of the neighborhood population is living below federal poverty levels and unemployment is almost 10%. About one-third of the family households with children are single-mother homes. The neighborhood is about 65% Latino, and 50% of the population are immigrants. The largest national origins are Puerto Rican, Mexican, Dominican, and Chinese. There are also families from almost every other country in Latin America. Almost 25% of adults over 25 years old have had some high school education but have not attained a high school diploma or equivalency, and more than 20% of the population have only completed eighth grade or below. Although these numbers may be high as a result of the large immigrant population, they are indicative of a community that has not had long-term emphasis on education. The area immediately surrounding the school may have a higher Latino percentage than the neighborhood as a whole, as indicated by the student population, which is 90% Latino. About 26% of the students are bilingual or English Language Learners.

Culturally Relevant Teaching

When I began thinking about using texts and materials that were culturally relevant to my students, I quickly had to figure out what *cultural relevance* is.

In the most obvious way, culturally relevant texts are those that clearly align themselves with the ethnicity of the reader. So, in my classroom of almost entirely Latino students, it meant reading literature by and about Latino people. However, this was too limiting and did not take into account the many other differences and cultural identities in my classroom or in the students' communities. For example, Dominicans and Puerto Ricans often form separate identities, as do Guatemalans and Mexicans, recent immigrants and second or third generations, boys and girls, working class and middle class, and so forth. I would not be able to accommodate those entirely different, overlapping, multiple, and complex identities at the same time. As an expanded definition of culture, I borrow from Alvermann (2001, p. 678), that "culture is generally thought to include the routines, artifacts, values, and concerns that people produce, make meaning of, and share as they work communally with others in their group." She is quick to point out, however, that there is no single way to be within a culture, that individual difference does exist. The best that I would be able to do in terms of providing materials would be to bring in as much as possible from as many different cultures, sources, ways of thinking, and so on. This also made sense because although the community surrounding the school is predominantly Latino, the rest of the city represents a diversity of many cultures and ways of thinking.

Learning About My Students. The other thing I realized was that the best way to understand my students' different cultures and personal interests (and plan accordingly) would be to let them tell me. One assignment that students completed was a family banner. These banners included words and illustrations describing their family traditions, the activities they do together for fun, the members of their immediate and extended family, and what is important to their family. I also gave my students reading surveys to learn about their attitudes and reading habits. As mentioned previously, many indicated that reading for them was boring, and few indicated that they read for fun. My students also spent far more time watching TV in a day than reading. Many stated that the purpose for reading was to become a better reader and to learn new things. In most of what I did with them, therefore, I started out with the assumption that my students had rich prior cultural knowledge, and that they would need to activate that in order to be receptive to learning for their own purposes.

Student Reading Assessments. In addition to finding texts that were relevant to my students' lives, it was also important to determine my students' instructional reading levels and to learn what strategies they employed to make sense of texts. I realized that many of my sixth-grade students read below grade level and often shut down as readers because of the difficulty of the text. At the beginning of the year I used our school system's informal reading assessments to assess each of my students. The assessments included graded word lists, a short oral reading passage, and comprehension questions. I took a running record to analyze student miscues and assessed comprehension through questioning and their retellings.

Developing a Sense of Community. Simultaneously, I worked to create a classroom environment in which students viewed themselves as part of a small community in that room, where each voice was heard, respected, and learned from. As Kong and Fitch (2002, p. 355) explain, "it was essential to create a learning community in which . . . culturally and linguistically diverse students would value the prior knowledge of their peers and thus feel psychologically safe to share personal experiences." To this end, I implemented a weekly class meeting, every last period on Friday. I established the two expectations I had for meetings: that everything said was to be kept in the room and respected, and that only one person would speak at a time. Each week, students shared their highs and lows of the week, reviewed the last week's meeting, and participated in one or two community-building activities. Students were also given an opportunity to bring up classroom issues.

My own identity as the primary classroom teacher was also worth considering when looking at the relationships I worked to establish with my students. As a white woman teacher, I was an outsider to the community, while at the same time a common sight in school. As a young teacher, I may have found ways to connect with my students and gain their respect. Furthermore, because I could speak and write in Spanish, I was able to quickly establish easy communication with parents. I sensed that this was a surprise and relief to many of my students and Spanish-speaking parents.

Culturally Relevant Teaching in the Literacy Block. Our class had a double-period literacy block in the morning, following homeroom. We were able to have a smooth transition from the business of homeroom into our read-aloud. The school followed the balanced literacy approach to reading and writing. These two components were given equal attention. Components of balanced literacy included a daily read-aloud; a mini-lesson, in which a skill or strategy is taught; and work time, which can be independent, partner, or small-group activities, during which the teacher provides extra support to students in need and conferences with students daily. In my classroom, the 90-minute block ended with a whole-group share of the thoughts, strategies used, and products of work time. We alternated daily between reading workshop and writing workshop. Fridays were often used for skills practice such as grammar or vocabulary.

For the first 6 weeks of school, I modeled ways of responding to a text, both orally and in writing. We practiced discussion using accountable talk, in which students listen to their peers and respond, add on, paraphrase, or bring up new ideas. I also modeled a method of journal response in which students first chose from a list of directed questions to guide their response, and then answered the question "What were you thinking as you were reading?" Throughout this time, we practiced strategies for dealing with unfamiliar words and providing support from the text in written and oral responses. During read-aloud, I read books such as *The House on Mango Street*, by Sandra Cisneros.

During a unit on characterization, we practiced making predictions and understanding character traits as well as characters' motivations. Students broke into smaller book club groups, reading the same book as several other students. I had a group of struggling readers read *Taking Sides*, by Gary Soto, a novel about a Mexican-American middle schooler who moves from his inner-city school to a suburban school. He plays basketball for his new team, and his loyalty is torn. Not only does the story tell of a Mexican-American kid; it is also the story of a boy who loves basketball. This high-interest, low-readability book was one that I selected with Juan in mind.

We also completed a nonfiction unit on editorials. I exposed students to a range of editorial articles, many of which were subjects students were familiar with, including articles about overcrowded schools, athlete salaries, school uniforms, and video games. After exposure to many editorials, students began their own editorials by brainstorming about things they felt passionate about. Using their own passions, interests, and opinions as a starting point, they created arguments to support their opinions. They then came up with possible counter-arguments and responses. They considered people they could interview to add support to their opinions. Throughout the writing project, students shared their arguments and got peer feedback about the strength of their arguments.

In a final unit of the study, students again responded to short stories they read. Read-alouds during this unit came from *145th Street*, a short story collection by Walter Dean Myers, and *Baseball in April and Other Stories;* a short story collection by Gary Soto. Our lessons focused on the story elements (setting, characters, plot, problem, and solution), and making personal connections to those elements in order to be able to understand and enjoy a text more. During reading time, I gave students copies of several short stories, including "Eleven," by Sandra Cisneros, "The Other Side," by Jacqueline Woodson, "A Chair for my Mother," by Vera Williams, "The Paper Bag Princess," by Robert Munsch, and "The Marble Champ," by Gary Soto. The stories deal with a variety of themes, including being 11 years old, racism and boundaries, family and poverty, friendship, and determination. After reading each story, students shared their immediate reactions and connections to the story with a partner. They then completed a "quick write" in their writer's notebooks, explaining the connection they made to the text.

As we moved through the units of study, I collected my own running observations and kid-watching notes during class discussions and conferencing to study my students' progress as readers and writers. I noted the specific skill (i.e., text connections, author's purpose) that was addressed in the observation. I used running charts to document the type of activity that was going on and where these occurred (partner discussion, student-teacher conferencing, whole group share, read-aloud, etc.).

Every night, students responded to texts and activities in their Reading Response Journals (RRJs). I checked student journals each day and collected copies of those that provided documentation to monitor their progress. Aside from daily RRJ entries, I collected writer's notebook entries and "published" writing pieces from students at the end of each unit of study. Finally, as part of the celebration for publishing, students read each other's pieces and gave written feedback. I collected these writings too.

The first major writing assignment, in which students were introduced to the writing process—brainstorming/seed collection, growing and selecting seed ideas, drafting, revising, and editing—was a personal narrative, in which students wrote on a short, important event in their lives. During the characterization unit, responses in RRJs and class discussions focused on understanding characters in our reading and on providing supporting evidence from the text. As a culminating writing piece for this unit, students read "The Gold Coin," by Alma Flor Ada. They wrote responses to the main character, his changes, and the reasons behind his changes, and practiced using textual support. In the editorial unit, students produced their own editorial on a topic of their choice. Their articles included more than one argument in support of their opinion, as well as a counter-opinion and response. In the final unit, students chose one of the stories we read in class (or were given the option of using a different short story), and expanded the quick write into a full essay. They were encouraged to take out a big idea or theme from the story that went beyond the story's details and could be applied to their own life.

 ## Literacy Challenges: Learner and Teacher

In the beginning, I focused more on my relationship with Juan and on his social and behavioral adjustment in my classroom. Early on, I saw no marked changes or attempts on his part to become a more active part of our learning community. In the first couple of months, his understanding of character traits, motivations, and relationships was fairly weak. His assessments of characters were superficial, dealing mainly with physical traits and momentary character emotions rather than enduring traits.

It was only when we were taking a break from reading to focus on a writing unit that he began a noticeable change. We were involved in a unit on personal narratives, as a way to get students to realize that they have stories to tell. This opportunity was one that I had hoped Juan would find appealing, since the few times that he had participated in the past occurred when he could share something from his personal experience. I noticed that he was not writing anything in his writer's notebook in our class writing sessions. However, on several occasions during writing time, he raised his hand and motioned for me to come over to him. He complained that he didn't know what to write. I saw this as a step for Juan, because previously he had not seemed to agonize or care at all if a period passed without a product; instead, he talked to the classmates around him and made disruptive noises and movements. The first time Juan wrote steadily during writing time was after one of my conferences with him. He said he had chosen to write his narrative about the day he got his father's teddy bear as a gift. I asked him to tell me about that day, and include everything he could remember. I reminded him to use his five senses and try to get every detail of those few minutes into the front of his head. After talking to me, he reverted to, "I don't know what to write," and "But I can't do this." I told him to write all the things he just told me, and not to worry about spelling and grammar at this time.

A few minutes later, Juan again called me over and asked, "Is this good?" I read what he wrote and asked more questions, probing for details and emotions about the day. By the end of the period, he had doubled his journal entry. During the next writing time, Juan left his desk and took a seat in the back of the room where he was not near other students. After a while, he was able to write steadily during most writing times, and his disruptions during class had become fewer and less angry. It was also during this time that Juan began participating in voluntary class meeting activities, such as discussions on the highs and lows of the week and other group shares.

Juan now chose to participate. We made it past a rocky start and began to see a classroom environment that had a place for his ideas and voice. He changed from avoiding writing to *wanting* to write and wanting to get my approval. Juan became a part of the classroom community, both as a social member and as an academic member.

 ## Addressing the Challenges

My next step was to flood him and our classroom in general with various culturally relevant texts to use for independent, partner, and whole-group work. When Juan began reading *Taking Sides*, by Gary Soto, his enthusiasm grew. On parent-teacher conferences, he told his mother that he had started reading a book "about a Latino kid." On the first day of in-class reading of this book, he refused to put it away when the period ended. Juan was in a small group of struggling readers, all assigned to read this book. He took on a leadership role in the group, starting discussion by explaining what he enjoyed about the book.

On December 15, I recorded that Juan said, "This book is like real life because Lincoln is a normal kid who plays basketball." By February, Juan was regularly participating in class discussions. He was eager to volunteer answers and at times even asked me before the discussion if he could share what he thought, "reserving" talking time. After he received his mid-year report card, Juan told me that it was his goal to make it onto the Honor Roll Board that year.

Although Juan was showing a much higher level of motivation in class, his homework habits were not reflecting this. He still lacked follow-through on completion of tasks that did not get done in class. On one occasion he mentioned that he had discussed his homework with his dad and had gotten some suggestions from him. Otherwise, there was no indication that he was sharing his work with his family. It was hard for me to tell if there was any transference at all from his enthusiasm in class when reading to his larger reading habits. For example, when students were assigned to complete the last few chapters of *Taking Sides* over winter vacation and to write a prompted essay, Juan did neither. A couple of months later, I asked Juan to finish the book. He picked it up and responded in his journal to it a few times, and then stopped. At that point, the task of rereading the chapters he had forgotten about, without the support he had had before, may have been a daunting task. He also began to read *Monster*, by Walter Dean Myers, but did not finish it. He still had not completed a book in its entirety since he arrived in my class in September.

Supporting Ideas with Evidence from the Text

Despite Juan's sporadic work habits, his comprehension skills when working with culturally relevant texts had clearly improved. Because Juan's early comments on texts often consisted of unsure statements that used words such as "maybe" and "probably" with little support from the text or any other logical source, I pushed him to provide evidence. He first began to do this through predictions or "wonderings" about what he read. For example, in a December 18th RRJ entry about an argument between two friends in *Taking Sides*, he wrote:

> I wonder if Lincoln is going to be friend's with Tony. Because Lincoln has the courage to stand up to Tony. Because Tony want to rob the thrift shop. Because the owner of the shop has his T.V. And Tony thought it was the right time to rob the owner, so then Lincoln stood up and told him to stop.

Here, Juan used the details from the story to explain why the friends had argued, and then logically wondered if they would become friends again.

Although Juan seemed to be very comfortable making predictions (he had written 12 journal entries focusing on this), he rarely went back to review the outcomes, even though I wrote notes to him in his RRJ to let me know in his next entry if his prediction was correct. Also, while showing logical thought and using evidence from the text in his predictions, he had still not begun to use textual evidence to make his own definitive statements about what he had already read, rather than what he'd be likely to find out as he continued to read. It was almost as if wonderings and predictions were a "safe" realm because the answer to the wondering had yet to be determined, and being wrong in a prediction was an acceptable possibility. I pushed him to move beyond predictions.

Connecting Personally to the Text

The next step that Juan took was to make text connections. At first, he had difficulty writing down his connections, saying that he had none. When I asked, however, if there was anything in the story that reminded him of something else, he was able to tell me exactly what part of the story he connected to. In conferences, I questioned him further about the connections he made, asking for more information and big connecting ideas. He was able to effectively explain his connection. When I then told him to write down what he had just explained to me, he had much less difficulty. He soon gained independence in writing text connections down without having to explain them orally first.

By showing personal connections to the text or relating a text to something else he had read about, he showed a broader view of his comprehension of texts. Also, it was when he began to connect to texts in some way (through himself or another text), that reading (and school in general) started seeming more meaningful and interesting to him, and less of a chore. Most of the connections he made were personal, such as, "This reminds me of when I moved to a new neighborhood and I didn't know anyone . . . ." He later made text-to-text connections. After reading the short story "The Other Side," Juan remarked that this story was like *Maniac McGee*, a novel by Jerry Spinelli, "because there were two sides of town."

Around the same time, he began retelling stories using accurate details from the text and including characters' names in his retell, rather than referring to characters as "this girl" or "some kid." In early March, after a silent reading of "The Other Side," he retold the plot to his partner by explaining that, "Clover's mom says not to go to the other side of the fence." Referring to the same story, he mentioned, "It was easy to go back and find evidence because I could relate to this story." I asked if he would mind sharing with the class what he had discovered about his reading process when he could relate to the story. He was eager to do this and seemed proud of the discovery.

Juan as an Active Reader, Thinker, and Writer

Juan also began to be able to draw logical conclusions, citing the text, about the author's purpose for including certain details. In early March, after finishing Walter Dean Myers's story "Big Joe's Funeral" as a read-aloud, I asked the class why they thought the author gave a light-hearted, funny story such a sad ending.

Several students gave possible reasons without supporting their thinking with story details. Juan raised his hand and said, "Like the author explained at the end, he was showing that even though there were some good times, life was still hard on 145th Street." Not only did he logically explain a choice the author had made, he had also clearly paraphrased the author's words to show his own comprehension of a large idea in this story. He applied details from the story to a broader message. This was a breakthrough moment for Juan, because he made a confident statement without relying on the uncertainty of a prediction or a personal connection as validation.

In February, students finished writing their final editorials. They rotated around the room in a peer share, giving them the opportunity to read and respond to each other's published pieces. After reading an article, they completed a peer review sheet, in which they pulled out the different points used in the argument, noting what was strong and what could be improved. Juan was able to systematically list the points made by the student author of the essay he read, as well as the counterargument. He also wrote to the author that he noticed she interviewed three people, and that "they all support her argument" and that he liked the way she "got support for her main idea." He pointed out a part in her paper that he felt needed to be clearer. He applied his understanding of main idea and supporting details as a reader in a critique of a classmate's writing. As a writer, this understanding was also evident. In his own editorial, he argued that people should eat less junk food. After his introduction, he supplied several specific health reasons to back up his argument. He seemed to have attained an awareness of these strategies that he could apply toward better comprehension and stronger writing.

Juan was using textual evidence to support his comprehension of texts in ways other than prediction and text connections. By the end of March, he looked below the surface of texts to draw conclusions based on textual evidence. For example, he explained that the details about a mother and a daughter playing tricks on each other in Gary Soto's "Mother and Daughter" showed that they had a close relationship. In a final writing project of the year, in which students made personal meaning out of a story of their choice, Juan wrote about Soto's "The Marble Champ." In a conference with him during writer's workshop, he explained to me that the main character, Lupe, did a good job at something he felt girls normally don't do—playing marbles. He said this showed that people can be good at things that other people say they shouldn't be good at, and this could apply to many types of situations. In his essay he wrote,

> Lupe is trying to tell you that you can do whatever you want to do. Don't do what other people tell you to do . . . . Be you. My life is similar to the girl's life because my sister be telling me I can't do this, can't do that.

He had combined strategies to be able to connect to the text he read, find a larger theme from it, and provide examples both from the text and from his own life.

Although in Juan's first tries at many of the comprehension strategies we tried he seemed more comfortable if he could run his ideas by me orally before committing them to writing, he later seemed to gain confidence in making statements without my approval. Sometimes, I would suggest that he tell his neighbor his idea instead of telling me, discuss it, and then write it down. When he did share his statements about texts with me first, I pushed him to provide more information and support by frequently asking him "Why?" His later demonstrations—both oral and written—of elaborating on his ideas about a text and providing evidence without being reminded indicate that he may have grown accustomed to this as a way of exploring what he had read, making it meaningful for himself and expanding his comprehension.

 ## Fitting Instruction to Meet the Needs of the Child

Overall, Juan's academic year was mixed. He clearly behaved differently and responded positively when offered text that was of cultural relevance to him. He also showed stronger comprehension skills when reading these texts. In school, he was changing positively, demonstrating an enthusiasm, persistence, and understanding that I had not previously seen. Out of school, this change was not as evident, shown by his lack of follow-through on homework assignments and completion of assignments begun in class and finished at home.

Juan showed heightened motivation and comprehension when presented with culturally relevant reading material. Still, throughout the study, I found it difficult to let go of a nagging question: Does this mean he can show he is a better reader on his citywide test in April? Despite my distaste for standardized testing as the primary assessment tool for my students (and, in many ways, the primary shaper of a struggling reader's academic self-esteem), I often feel stuck within a framework that *does* place such value on the score from this test. Like it or not, Juan's promotion to seventh grade depended mostly on a test that has few, if any, truly culturally relevant text selections in it.

Through a conversation with other colleagues, I was able to come to terms with the possibility that his higher level of performance in our class would not necessarily show itself on the test. If students are progressing in my classroom, even if it means simply that they are reading more and seeing themselves as readers, then they are far more likely to progress as readers in general.

Reading things we feel strongly about or enjoy is what makes us read and become better readers. Without the ongoing opportunity for a struggling reader to read material that he/she chooses or is passionate about, how can we expect a struggling reader to improve? So, because the test is *not* authentic for most students and is not the be-all, end-all of good reading, it is worth providing an environment in which readers, fluent or struggling, can progress. Providing culturally relevant texts for students involved creating a classroom that respected cultural differences and that was built up from students' individual and unique experiences. With this focus, I was forced to abandon assumptions about my students' cultures and allow them to dictate their interests and backgrounds to me. For example, sometimes finding a culturally relevant text required finding sports-themed writing that also included Latino characters.

Juan may have made it to sixth grade without ever having been exposed to literature relevant to his life, and although there is no way to know, I wonder if his identity as a reader would have been different had this not happened. This is not to say that it is too late for Juan—or for a struggling reader in any grade. On the contrary, it is to say that opening up new literature possibilities for a student can change a child's approach to reading and perhaps even school. At the same time, it is my hope that teachers of younger students might use this approach as well.

References

Ada, A. F. (1991). *The Gold Coin*. U.S.A.: Del Sol.

Alvermann, D. (2001). Reading adolescents' reading identities: Looking back to see ahead. *Journal of Adolescent and Adult Literacy, 44*(8), 676–690.

Cisneros, S. (1991). *The house on Mango Street*. New York: Vintage.

Cisneros, S. (1992). *Woman Hollering Creek and other stories*. New York: Vintage.

Gambrell, L. B. (1996). Creating classroom cultures that foster reading motivation. *The Reading Teacher, 50*(1), 14–25.

Jordan, L., & Hendricks, C. (2002). Increasing sixth grade students' engagement in literacy learning. *Networks: An Online Journal for Teacher Research, 5*(1). Retrieved October 2007 from http://journals.library.wise.edu/index.php/networks/article/view/ 151/156.

Kong, A., & Fitch, E. (2002). Using Book Club to engage culturally and linguistically diverse learners in reading, writing, and talking about books. *Reading Teacher, 56*(4), 352–362.

Munsch, R. (1992). *The paper bag princess*. Toronto: Annick.

Myers, W. D. (2000). *145th Street: Short Stories*. New York: Dell Laurel-Leaf.

Myers, W. D. (1999). *Monster*. New York: Scholastic.

Soto, G. (1990). *Baseball in April and other stories*. New York: Harcourt.

Soto, G. (2003). *Taking sides*. New York: Harcourt.

Spinelli, J. (1990). *Maniac McGee*. New York: Scholastic.

U.S. Census Bureau. (2007). *American Fact Finder; people; generated on April 7, 2004, by zip code;* from http://factfinder.census.gov/servlet/SAFFPeople?geo_id=&_geoContext=&_street=&_county=&_cityTown=&_state=&_zip=&_lang=en&_sse=on.

Williams, V.B. (1982). *A chair for my mother*. Hong Kong: Harper.

Woodson, J. (2001). *The other side*. New York: Putnam.

Afterword

What makes us effective literacy teachers? The solution begins with our shared belief that we are responsible for teaching each learner to reach his or her full potential (Allington, 1991). Secondly, we value listening to our students to connect our teaching to what they know, to respond to their needs, and to support their successful engagement as readers, writers, and communicators. We also recognize that we do not always have answers, but may negotiate literacy challenges by engaging in a cycle of assessment, instruction, and reflection. Blair, Rupley, and Nichols (2007) reviewed the literature over the past 20 years to offer common features of effective teachers of reading. Our stories also exhibit these features. Their list includes:

1. assessing students' reading strengths and weaknesses,
2. structuring reading activities around an explicit instructional format,
3. providing students with opportunities to learn and apply skills and strategies in authentic reading tasks,
4. ensuring that students attend to the learning tasks, and
5. believing in one's teaching abilities and expecting students to be successful. (p. 433).

We invite you to share your stories. Consider writing them down as we did or keeping a teacher journal to be shared during a study group for reflective practice and teacher research. Below is the framework we used to guide our inquiries.

Identify a Learner
- Choose a learner you would like to study.
- What literacy challenges do you notice?
- What do you know about your learner as a person?

Knowing Where to Begin
- What literacy assessments might help you to learn more about your learner's challenges?
- What does the professional literature and research offer?
- What do others know about this learner?

Literacy Challenges: Teacher and Learner

- Describe your instruction.
- How are you measuring student progress and what do these assessments tell you?
- What are your challenges?

Addressing the Challenge

- How have you changed your instruction to meet the needs and progress of your learner?

Fitting Instruction to Meet the Needs of the Learner

- Reflect on the teaching-learning journey. What did you learn about your student? What did you learn about yourself as a teacher?

References

Allington, R. L. (1991). Children who find learning to read difficult: School responses to diversity. In E. H. Hiebert (Ed.), *Literacy for a diverse society: Perspectives, practices, and social policies* (pp. 237–252). New York: Teachers College Press.

Blair, T. R., Rupley, W. H., & Nichols, W. D. (2007). The effective teacher of reading: Considering the "what" and "how" of instruction. *The Reading Teacher, 60,* 432–438.